Handbook of Comparative Education Law

Books Previously Published by Charles J. Russo

Primer on Legal Affairs for the School Business Official
Key Legal Issues for Schools: The Ultimate Resource for School Business Officials
The Educational Rights of Students: International Perspectives on Demystifying the Legal Issues
What's the Harm? Does Legalizing Same-Sex Marriage Really Harm Individuals, Families or Society?
The Employment Rights of Teachers: Exploring Education Law Worldwide
The Law of Special Education and Non-Public Schools: Major Challenges in Meeting the Needs of Youth with Disabilities
God vs. Darwin: The War between Evolution and Creationism in the Classroom
The Legal Rights of Students with Disabilities: International Perspectives
Key Legal Issues for Schools: The Ultimate Resource for School Business Officials, 2nd Edition
Handbook of Comparative Higher Education Law
Global Interest in Student Behavior: An Examination of International Best Practices, Volume 1
International Perspectives on Student Behavior: What We Can Learn, Volume 2
Gravissimum Educationis: Golden Opportunities in American Catholic Education 50 Years after Vatican II
Handbook of Comparative Education Law: British Commonwealth Nations, Volume 1

Forthcoming books by Charles J. Russo

Schools and Religion
Religion in American Education: A Legal Encyclopedia
Handbook of Comparative Education Law: Selected European Nations, Volume 3
Handbook of Comparative Education Law: The Americas and Selected African Nations, Volume 4
Student Discipline: An International Problem
The Law of Special Education: A Hands-On Guide for Educators and Parents

Handbook of Comparative Education Law

Selected Asian Nations, Volume 2

Edited by Charles J. Russo

ROWMAN & LITTLEFIELD
Lanham • Boulder • New York • London

Published by Rowman & Littlefield
A wholly owned subsidiary of
The Rowman & Littlefield Publishing Group, Inc.
4501 Forbes Boulevard, Suite 200, Lanham, Maryland 20706
https://rowman.com

Unit A, Whitacre Mews, 26-34 Stannary Street, London SE11 4AB,
United Kingdom

British Library Cataloguing in Publication Information Available

Library of Congress Cataloging-in-Publication Data

Names: Russo, Charles J., editor.
Title: Handbook of comparative education law. Volume 2, Selected Asian nations / edited by Charles J. Russo.
Description: Lanham : Rowman & Littlefield, [2017] | Includes bibliographical references and index.
Identifiers: LCCN 2017031629 (print) | LCCN 2017032922 (ebook) | ISBN 9781475839555 (Electronic) | ISBN 9781475839531 (cloth : alk. paper) | ISBN 9781475839548 (pbk. : alk. paper)
Subjects: LCSH: Educational law and legislation--Asia.
Classification: LCC KNC720 (ebook) | LCC KNC720 .H36 2017 (print) | DDC 344.5/07--dc23
LC record available at https://lccn.loc.gov/2017031629.

∞ ™ The paper used in this publication meets the minimum requirements of American National Standard for Information Sciences Permanence of Paper for Printed Library Materials, ANSI/NISO Z39.48-1992.

Printed in the United States of America

Contents

Acknowledgments ix

Introduction xi

1 China 1
Ran Zhang and Jinju Yao

2 Israel 27
Dan Gibton

3 Palestine 53
Akram Daoud and Lucy Royal-Dawson

4 Republic of Korea 81
Jang Wan Ko, Sheena Choi, and Hyowon Park

5 Turkey 103
Ricardo Lozano and Irem Comoğlu

6 Analysis and Reflections 123
Charles J. Russo

Index 135

About the Editor 141

About the Contributors 143

Acknowledgments

As with any book, there are a number of people who must be thanked. Four sets of people in were very helpful in assisting me in putting this book together. First, many thanks to Tom Koerner, Vice President and Editorial Director at Rowman & Littlefield Education, who was most supportive of this project from its inception through its being published. Thanks also to Ms. Emily Tuttle, an associate editor, and Mr. Chris Fischer, an assistant production editor, for copyediting the text.

Second, it almost goes without saying that I am most grateful to the authors for their valuable contributions to this book.

Third, I would like to thank my assistant, Ms. Elizabeth Pearn at the University of Dayton, for her efforts in copyediting and helping to prepare the final manuscript for publication.

At the University of Dayton, I would like to thank my Dean in the School of Education and Health Sciences, Kevin Kelly, my chair in the Department of Educational Administration, Dave Dolph, and my dean in the School of Law, Andrew Strauss, for their ongoing support and encouragement as well as for providing an atmosphere which is conducive to ongoing research and academic inquiry.

Fourth, but certainly not least, I would like to express my deepest appreciation for my wife Debbie, my daughter Emily, and our granddaughter Lorelai, to whom this book is dedicated, for their ongoing love and support, without which none of this work would have been completed.

Introduction

As the world continues to shrink amid growing interdependence, one of the major challenges facing the global community is ensuring the establishment of sound, working school systems designed to produce educated citizenries. The law is a major factor that helps to create educational systems while monitoring their quality as it protects the rights of both teachers and students. Clearly, this is a daunting task for legal systems around the world as they seek to ensure national stability and well-educated citizenries.

The centrality of education on an international level was first highlighted by the promulgation of the Universal Declaration on Human Rights (Declaration) in 1948.[1] In fact, the Declaration was the first internationally accepted document to enunciate the value of education as a basic human right; this recognition has helped to shape not only the nature of school systems but has also helped to define and safeguard the rights of students, their parents, and teachers. According to Article 26 of this Declaration:

1. Everyone has the right to education. Education shall be free, at least in the elementary and fundamental stages. Elementary education shall be compulsory. Technical and professional education shall be made generally available and higher education shall be equally accessible to all on the basis of merit.
2. Education shall be directed to the full development of the human personality and to the strengthening of respect for human rights and fundamental freedoms. It shall promote understanding, tolerance and friendship among all nations, racial or religious groups, and shall further the activities of the United Nations for the maintenance of peace.
3. Parents have a prior right to choose the kind of education that shall be given to their children.

Additionally, a variety of other international and domestic documents, including judicial opinions of the United States Supreme Court and those of high courts in other nations, have recognized the rights not only of students to receive an education but also of the corresponding right addressing the freedom of teachers to teach as they deem fit, free from unwarranted governmental interference. At the same time, there has been incredible growth in the rate at which children attend school in developing nations, necessitating the creation of a body of well-educated teachers who can instruct these students.

Starting with the enactment of compulsory schooling laws for primary schools in the middle of the nineteenth century,[2] especially in Western industrialized nations beginning with the United States, enrollments in elementary and secondary education have grown dramatically. Even so, a 2010 analysis, published in 2013, of 146 nations reveals that among persons fifteen years of age and older in 1950, 47.1 percent lacked any formal education, a number that has declined to 14.55 percent.[3] Moreover, elementary school completion grew from only 17.1 percent to 17.3 percent while those who completed a secondary education did increase from 5.2 percent to 25.9 percent.[4] To this end, a study published by the World Bank noted that the patterns of educational attainment clearly vary greatly across various countries as well as across population groups within these nations.[5]

For some, basic education is practically universal, whereas for others attainment is dismal as the average years of study rose from only 3.12 to 7.89.[6] A value of this proposed volume, then, is that it is designed to provide users with an understanding of how laws in selected countries promote the development of educational systems that can be used in nations where schooling for all is still not a priority.

Concerns over the need for primary and secondary schools, let alone higher education, have emerged as important throughout the world, largely as a consequence of the increasing range of rights accorded citizens in their home countries. While there are similarities in the ways educational institutions operate, there are also many differences. Further, legislative and judicial systems around the world continue to draw increasingly on the knowledge and experience of educational leaders in other countries in order to improve on the quality of schooling in their own countries.

As the second of four books on comparative legal issues in education, this volume joins others I have edited alone or with others on the rights of students, teachers, children with disabilities, student discipline, and the status of higher education); then, this work focuses on issues in elementary or primary and secondary education so as to offer guidance to educational and legislative leaders in other nations.

This book and its companion volumes include original chapters addressing legal issues in nineteen countries on all six inhabited continents. All of the chapters follow the same template to facilitate the study of similarities and differences between and among countries. Even so, the authors were free to add information as they saw fit. All of the chapter authors are leading academicians in education law in the countries about which they have written and most have contributed to other volumes in this series on the rights of students and students with disabilities, the rights of teachers, the status of higher education, and disciplining of students in elementary and secondary schools, thereby enhancing a strong continuity from one volume to the next.

As such, insofar as the purpose of laws are concerned with developing educated citizenries starting with children, this book examines similarities and differences in education laws in China, Israel, Palestine, Turkey, and South Korea in the hope of enhancing international awareness of the similarities and advantages associated with bringing together knowledge from five countries concerning various issues in higher education. It is my hope to have this book serve as a valuable resource for academicians, lawyers, and educational practitioners by providing them with an enhanced awareness of strategies that are being used to manage problems commonly faced in multiple educational settings. The authors have taken every effort to demystify the legal complexities and technical language of the law as it related to education law education while ensuring that their work is reader friendly.

OVERVIEW OF THIS VOLUME

In light of the uneven status of the education laws in many places, this book includes essays by experts from five nations to address commonalities in this important, and timely, issue. These experts, all of whom are accomplished academics and/or jurists, are Ran Zhang and Jinju Yao, from China; Dan Gibton, from Israel; Akram Daoud of Palestine and Lucy Royal-Dawson (from Northern Ireland); Jang Wan Ko, Sheena Choi, and Hyowon Park from South Korea; and Ricardo Lozano now in Texas, formerly in Turkey, and Irem Comoğlu of Turkey.

The five nations examined in this volume were selected because they offer a good cross-section of the education law systems in the countries in the diverse regions of Asia. As the most populous nation in the world, China was a natural for inclusion in this book. Next, South Korea was included because it represents a stable democracy in Southeast Asia. Israel and Palestine were chosen because as neighbors in a volatile part of the world, it is worth looking at how they are similar yet different. Finally, Turkey was selected as a representative of a nation with an Islamic majority in which the educational system has been modeled largely after European models. Together, the education law systems in these five nations present interesting similarities and contrasts in the way they operate, based on the unique way in which their national heritages developed, thereby allowing for interesting analyses.

Based on a common outline, these experts examined such issues as the nature of their national legal systems, school governance models, instructional issues, the rights of students and teachers, and emerging issues. Acknowledging the ways in which issues vary from one nation to the next, especially in light of their cultural, religious, political, and practical differences, the authors examined the topics as they saw appropriate, presenting them from their own points of view.

By affording chapter authors some latitude as they address the identified topics, it is still possible to draw conclusions in a final chapter that can hopefully lead to future dialogue and study. Further, as noted, recognizing the importance of as far-reaching a representation as possible, I was fortunate to be able to ensure that I had at least one nation on each continent or region of the world represented in the two volumes. It is my fervent hope that this collection of essays will enhance a common understanding of the status of K–12 education throughout the world. As interdependence grows in a continually shrinking world, then one of the major challenges facing the global community is to observe what goes on in other nations as leaders seek to learn from one another in facing the challenge of preparing educated citizenries for the future.

Readers are advised that rather than translate all notes and other pertinent terms into English, they are occasionally transliterated in their original languages. I have done this not only because the underlying documents are often unavailable in English but also since translating text might create difficulties for native speakers who wish to research relevant materials. In addition, since each of the nations covered in this book uses slightly different systems of legal citation, I have left references in their original form rather than attempt to standardize them under one rubric. Finally, I have preserved minor variations in the different forms of English used throughout the world so that readers can get a flavor of how our seemingly common tongue is used throughout the world, particularly for scholars whose native language is not English.

CONCLUSION

Of course, no single book can ever hope to cover the myriad of legal topics, or laws of nations, addressing the legal status of K–12 education law. Even so, I hope that these informative, thought provoking, well written and researched chapters, authored by leading scholars in the field, can serve as up-to-date and ready sources of information to help keep educational leaders, academics, and students abreast of the many changes in the ever-growing area of comparative education law.

NOTES

1. Universal Declaration on Human Rights (1948), http://www.un.org/en/documents/udhr/index.shtml/.
2. C. J. Russo (2010). "Reflections on Education as a Fundamental Human Right," *Education and Law Journal*, Vol. 18, No. 1, 87–105.
3. R. J. Barro and J. W. Lee, (2013). "A New Data Set of Educational Attainment in the World, 1950–2010," *Journal of Development Economics*, *Vol. 104*, 184–198, table 3. See also World Bank (2009), Educational Attainment and Enrollment Around the World, http://web.worldbank.org/external/default/main?menuPK=1460753&pagePK=64168176&piPK=64168140&theSitePK=1460718#education.
4. Ibid.
5. World Bank (2009), Educational Attainment and Enrollment Around the World, http://web.worldbank.org/external/default/main?menuPK=1460753&pagePK=64168176&piPK=64168140&theSitePK=1460718#education.
6. Barro and Lee supra note 3.

Chapter One

China

Ran Zhang and Jinju Yao

INTRODUCTION

With its population of 1.3 billion, China has the largest elementary and secondary education system in the world. In 2014, there were 219,632 elementary schools, 53,993 lower secondary schools, and 25,677 upper secondary schools in China. The total number of students was about 182 million, and the total number of full-time teachers was about 11.7 million.[1] Protecting the rights of such a great number of students and faculty members is not only crucial for the maintenance of the education system itself but also important for the social and economic development of China and the world beyond.

China has adopted a 6-3-3 schooling system, with six years of elementary education, three years of lower secondary education, and three years of upper secondary education. Elementary and lower secondary education are compulsory. Although some elementary schools do operate kindergarten programs, they are neither a necessary component of elementary education nor is attendance compulsory. Upper secondary education is provided at both regular upper secondary schools and upper secondary vocational schools.

This chapter begins with a brief overview of the sources of education law in China. This overview sketches out a general picture of the hierarchy of education laws and highlights some constitutional and statutory foundations for school law in China. Next, it zooms in to analyze specific legal issues related to the school system, faculty rights, and student rights, which constitute the main body of the chapter. Taken together, these three sections provide a multifaceted landscape of elementary and secondary education law in China. The chapter concludes with a discussion of a few overarching themes in elementary and secondary education law in China.

LEGAL AND CONSTITUTIONAL SOURCES OF EDUCATION LAW

China is traditionally a code law country, but case law has begun to play an important role in recent years. The main sources of education law in China consist primarily of a hierarchical system of legal codes, including the Constitution, statutes, State Council regulations, provincial and local legislations, ministry regulations, legislations, and rules in the self-governing ethnic minority regions, and international covenants or conventions.

In recent years, case law has become more significant. The Supreme People's Court issued Provisions on Case Guidance in 2010 and Implementation Details regarding the Provisions on Case Guidance in 2015, requiring courts to refer to selected guiding cases in similar disputes. To date, two higher educational law cases have been designated as guiding cases.[2] Although both cases involved higher education, their underlying legal principles may be applicable to elementary and secondary schooling.

The Constitution proclaims both citizens' right to education and the state's responsibilities to establish schools. Insofar as the right to education clause is placed under the chapter of "Fundamental Rights and Duties of Citizens" in the Constitution,[3] there is no doubt that the right to education is a fundamental right of citizens in China. As noted the wording of the Constitution limits the right to education to Chinese citizens, suggesting that foreign children may not receive the same level of education.

Article 19 of the Constitution stipulates state responsibilities for establishing an education system: "The State runs schools of various types, makes primary education compulsory and universal, develops secondary, vocational and higher education and promotes pre-school education." It is important to note that the Constitution was initially passed in 1982 when compulsory education had not been formally established.

In light of the economic and social developments in China in recent decades, elementary and lower-secondary education has become compulsory and universal; upper-secondary education has become free in some cities or regions as it is supported by local government while vocational secondary education has made fee remission generally available to all students from rural areas or with low socioeconomic status.

The Constitution is highest authority in the legal hierarchy. Even so, the Education Law (1995) is the ultimate source of law within the field of education as it spells out the basic structure of the education system of China as well as the rights and duties of students, teachers, and schools. The Compulsory Education Law (1986), the Teachers Law (1993), the Vocational Education Law (1996), and the Law on the Promotion of Non-Public Schools (2002) address issues in their specific domains. Moreover, the Law on the Protection of Minors (2006), albeit not an education statute per se, contains many provisions related to minors' rights and the school's responsibilities for the protection of minors.

INSTITUTIONAL ISSUES

Compulsory Education

In China, children who have reached the age of six must attend school for nine years in elementary and lower-secondary education.[4] Children of school age, their parents, or other legal guardians, related social organizations, and individuals all have the duty to enable students to finish compulsory education.[5] Child labor is prohibited in China.[6] Parents or legal guardians have the responsibility to provide necessary conditions for the education of minors. If parents fail to send children to school, government officials can reprimand them and order compliance within set periods.[7]

This school attendance requirement can be satisfied by private schools, but whether it can be met by home schooling has been a controversial in recent years. From the wording of the law, homeschooling appears to be illegal for children of compulsory education age. Article 11 of the Compulsory Education Law stipulates, "his/her parents or other statutory guardians shall have him/her enrolled in school to finish compulsory education." However, out of dissatisfaction with public education, a significant number of parents have opted to home educate their children[8] by founding a national liaison group for homeschooling.[9]

Funding for Public Education

Corresponding to the notion of compulsory school attendance is the government's responsibility to provide public education. Compulsory education is free in China.[10] Funding for public education comes from the local government, but the provincial and the central government provide special funding support for rural education, especially for less developed areas.[11]

The Education Law also sets forth required increases with regard to education finance. For example, the proportion of government educational appropriation in gross national product (GNP) should gradually increase as the national economy develops and the fiscal revenue rises.[12] Governments at all levels shall ensure that their educational appropriations increases at a faster rate than their regular revenues, that the average expenditures spent on each enrolled student increase steadily, and that teachers' salaries and average public expenditure per student should increase steadily.[13]

Public-private partnerships (PPP) have become an emerging feature in school financing. Vouchers have been used in some places to fund preschool education,[14] vocational education,[15] and students with low socioeconomic status.[16] It is fairly common for local governments to purchase early childhood education from private preschools. In addition, in the process of integrating information technology into school curricula, officials in some public schools have purchased services from private companies.[17]

Administration System

The Ministry of Education, the highest education authority in China, is in charge of overall planning, coordination, and management of educational undertakings throughout the country. The Department of Education at the provincial level and educational bureaus at city and county levels are in charge of educational work in their respective areas.[18]

When the National People's Congress, the State Council, and/or the Ministry of Education issues legal rulings, provincial and local education agencies are bound to observe and implement it. Yet the state usually leaves special issues in elementary and secondary education to the governance of provincial and lower levels of government.[19] In the compulsory education stage, the provincial government is responsible for overall planning under the leadership of the State Council while the county-level government is mainly responsible for administration.[20]

Types of Schools

Vocational schools

In China, vocational education is governed by the Vocational Education Law (1996). On graduation from lower secondary schools, students may choose to enroll in a vocational education schools as a form of upper secondary education.[21] While general upper secondary school education may offer some vocational education classes,[22] vocational education delivery mainly takes the form of specialized vocational upper-secondary schools and vocational colleges.

Compulsory education in China does not cover upper-secondary education. Even so, the state currently provides tuition grants to vocational education students if they come from very poor rural areas, if they major in agriculture-related fields, or if they come from families with low socioeconomic status. This policy is designed to promote both vocational education and equity.[23]

Private Schools

Private schools are regulated by the Law on the Promotion of Non-Public Schools (2002). In China, private schools are called *minban* schools, whereas the word *minban* literally means people-run so as to be distinguished from state-run public schools as state-run. Social organizations, private businesses, and individuals can all establish private schools.[24] Private schools are supposed to share equal legal status with public schools and have autonomy in school operation.[25] Unlike public schools, which do not always have independent legal status, private schools must be registered as independent legal persons (*faren*) so as to bear all their liabilities on their own properties.

Private schools are subject to state regulations and public supervision. Like public schools, private schools can only hire teachers who have earned licenses.[26] Due to the strict separation of religion and education, religious private schools are not allowed.[27] Further, private schools need to send their recruitment bulletins and advertisements to the relevant educational administrative agencies for documentation.[28] Educational administrative agencies may also send proctors to private schools and conduct, or can commission nongovernment organizations to carry out, evaluations on the quality of teaching in private schools.[29]

For a long time, for-profit private schools were not officially allowed in China.[30] However, the law is likely to change soon. In the past, despite the prohibition of profit making, the law allows for a "reasonable return" (*heli huibao*) from the cash surplus from school operations to be extracted to the persons or organizations funding schools, after the costs of school operations are deducted, the funds for school development are withheld, and the sum of money for other necessary expenses is drawn in accordance with the relevant regulations of the state.[31] In such situations, private schools are no longer qualified for receiving the same level of tax exemptions or other beneficial policies which public and not-for-reasonable-return private higher education institutions would enjoy.[32]

The legal design of "reasonable return" is supposed to encourage private investment in education. In practice, though, few private school investors have claimed this reasonable return even though many of them do get their investments back. In other words, the legal design becomes a dead letter in its actual implementation.

At the end of 2015, the Education Law was already amended to drop provisions against profit-seeking schools. Currently, the Law on the Promotion of Non-Public Schools is also under revision. It is likely in the near future that both nonprofit and for-profit private schools will be allowed in China with the two types of schools corresponding to different tax benefit structures, different accounting rules, and different claims to the remaining properties after liquidation.

International Schools

Broadly speaking, there are three types of "international schools" in China: schools for children of foreign diplomats (*waijiao renyuan zinv xuexiao*), schools for children of foreign personnel (*waiji renyuan zinv xuexiao*), and Sino-China cooperation schools (*zhongwai hezuo banxue*).

The first type of school recruits children of foreign diplomats. State law recognizes the existence of these schools but does not provide any regulations.[33] The second type of school type recruits children of foreigners living in China. The establishment of such schools needs to be approved by relevant provisional education agencies. These schools can design their own curricula. As a form of supervision, the state law requires such schools to send their faculty roster, student roster, and textbooks to local educational agencies for documentation and to be subject to supervision visits.[34]

While the first and the second types of schools can recruit only children with foreign passports,[35] the third type of "international schools" targets mainly children with Chinese passports. This third type, officially called "Chinese-foreign cooperative schools," is jointly established by Chinese and foreign educational institutions.[36] State law requires such schools to offer some citizenship education curricula and to send both their curricula and textbooks to the approval agency for documentation.[37] Such cooperative schools can be established on the levels of early childhood education, upper-secondary education, and post-secondary education, but not on the level of compulsory education.[38]

In practice, some private schools, although not officially recognized as international schools, offer internationally oriented curriculum such as International Baccalaureate Programs in addition to the mandated private school curriculum.[39] Many of the graduates of these schools aim to pursue their postsecondary education overseas. Once approved, such private schools can also recruit children with foreign passports. Therefore, such internationally oriented private schools, which are capable of serving students at the compulsory education stage, may function like de facto international schools.

Safety and Liability Issues

As to the liability of schools for students' injuries, the doctrine of in loco parentis was rejected in China.[40] Instead, school officials have the general responsibility for educating and managing (*jiaoyu yu guanli*) students. Unless otherwise specified in law, negligence is a necessary condition for school liability.[41] The general tort law logic is applicable to student accidents in school. But for students below the age of ten the burden of proof is on the school's side. Put another way, school officials would be liable if they fail to prove that they have fulfilled their duties of education and management when a student is injured.[42]

For students' injury resulting from the actions of outsiders such as campus crime conducted by third persons, the outside attackers are the primary liability bearers, and, if a school has flaws in its safety measure, it and its officials are the secondary liability bearers. With this so-called corresponding complementary liability, school authorities are liable only when primary liability bearers are incapable of paying for the full damages they caused. Yet, in such a situation, the law is unclear whether the school is then only responsible for its portion of the liabilities, or the "corresponding" part, or must take on all of the liabilities unpaid by the primary bearer or the "complementary" part.[43]

FACULTY RIGHTS

The Teachers Law (1993) defines the status of teachers as "professionals,"[44] which suggests that the employment rules, rights, and duties of civil servants do not necessarily apply to public school teachers. The same Teachers Law also stipulates that teachers' average salary shall not be lower than that of civil servants and shall be gradually raised. This legal design is supposed to attract talent into the teaching profession. This section provides a brief overview about licensure, employment issues, due process protection, substantive rights, union, and equal protection rights of elementary and secondary school teachers in China.

Licensure

Teacher licensure is a prerequisite for teaching in Chinese schools.[45] In order to obtain a teacher license, individuals must take the national teacher licensure test.[46] The national teacher licensure test is open to persons meeting the following four requirements: holding Chinese citizenship; complying with the Constitution, applicable laws, and standards for professional ethics; satisfying physical eligibility requirements; and attaining the relevant educational levels as specified in the Teachers Law.[47]

After passing all the components of the licensure test, applicants must apply for teacher licensure at the local educational agencies within three years.[48] Teachers are licensed based on the level of the school where they teach rather than on their subject areas or grade levels. Teachers with higher-level licenses are automatically eligible to teach at lower-level schools.[49]

Establishment of Employment

Teacher employment is established through employment contracts. Article 17 of the Teachers Law stipulates that "the school and the teacher shall sign an appointment contract defining each other's rights, obligations and responsibilities." In China, some public schools are independent legal persons (*duli faren*), which means that they can enter contacts under their own names. All registered private schools are independent legal persons. For public schools lacking independent legal status, employment contracts may be signed by officials of local educational agencies. In practice, even for public schools with independent legal status, employment contracts are often signed by officials of local educational agencies.

Employment contracts have become the norm even though public school teachers used to enjoy permanent employment. In the past, graduates from normal schools, colleges, and universities were assigned teaching jobs on graduation. Unless there was extraordinary neglect of duty, their employment was secure. After the personnel reform, permanent employment was replaced with term contracts even though a system of *bianzhi* still exits.

Bianzhi is like a formal recognition of public employee status. Public school teachers who have *bianzhi* sign personnel contracts with their school employers. Public school teachers who do not have *bianzhi* and private school teachers sign labor contracts with their schools. On average, teachers under personnel contracts have stronger job security and better benefits packages than those under labor contracts. Teachers also differ in terms of applicable laws. The Labor Contract Law (2007) is directly applicable to labor contracts but is used when dealing with personnel contracts only in the absence of relevant personnel laws or regulations.[50]

In light of the recent reform replacing previous permanent employment with term contracts, there is no tenure system for elementary and secondary school teachers in China.[51] However, some teachers may be eligible to sign contracts without fixed terms as a way to ensure their job security. For non-*bianzhi* holding teachers in public schools and those in private schools, if they have consecutively worked in the schools for ten years or have already signed and dutifully fulfilled two consecutive contracts with their schools, they have the right to ask their employers to sign contracts without termination dates. Under the Labor Contract Law,[52] employers shall sign such contracts. For public school teachers with *bianzhi*, if they have consecutively worked in their schools for ten years and there are less than ten years before their mandatory retirement ages,[53] they can ask school officials to sign contracts with the termination dates specified as their retirement dates.[54]

Teacher Ethics, Disciplinary Action, and Dismissal

Teacher ethics has been the target of many education policies in recent years. The Ministry of Education published professional ethical norms for elementary and secondary school teachers in 2008 and disciplinary measures in 2014.

Like two sides of the same coin, these two policies, coupled with scattered provisions in the Teachers Law, prohibit teachers from engaging in the following activities: classroom speech or conduct in conflict with policies of the state or the Chinese Communist Party; failure to protect the safety of students in the case of an emergency at school; unfair treatment or assessment of students, which has produced significant detrimental effects; falsification or corruption in student recruitment, student assessment, teacher evaluation, promotion, and publication of teaching or research outcomes; and corporal punishment of students, which has harmed students' physical or psychological well-being.

These policies also forbid sexual harassment of students or having an improper relationship with students; soliciting or accepting gifts or money from students or their parents; involvement in business activities targeting students or forcing students to subscribe to supplemental education materials; requiring students to receive paid tutoring service, organizing or teaching in tutoring companies; intentional educational malpractice; and other serious violations of professional ethics.[55]

Teachers violating the above rules may be subject to disciplinary actions, including warnings, demerits on their records, demotions or the removal of their professional titles, removals from administrative position, revocation of teacher licenses, and dismissal.[56] These disciplinary measures and the following due process protections apply to teachers in both public and private schools.[57]

In the disciplinary process including dismissal, teachers are entitled to due process protection. Before negative decisions are reached, officials in schools or local educational agencies shall give teachers opportunities to defend themselves, learn what students, other teachers, and parents think about their behavior, and notify them of their right to request hearings. For more severe disciplinary actions other than warnings and demerits on records, a policy of Ministry of Education policy mandates hearings.[58] After negative decisions, teachers can ask officials at local educational agencies to reconsider their cases. If they are still dissatisfied with the decisions, teachers may file appeals to the next upper level educational agencies.[59]

Substantive Rights

Article 7 of the Teachers Law specifies the following six main substantive rights of teachers: the right to teach, the right to research, the right to student management and student discipline, the right to receive salaries, benefits, and summer and winter breaks with pay, the right to participate in school management, and the right to continuing education.

First, "teachers have the right to conduct educational and instructional activities, reforms, and experiments."[60] In light of Article 35 of the Compulsory Education Law, while the Ministry of Education decides on teaching content and curricula, teachers are encouraged to explore and adopt appropriate instructional methods. So, the right to teach is mainly the right to select teaching methods.

Second, "teachers have the right to engage in scientific research and academic exchange, join professional academic societies, and fully express their views on academic activities."[61] Teachers have the right to academic freedom and freedom of association relevant to their work. However, as mentioned earlier in the section on teacher discipline, teachers are prohibited from classroom speeches or conduct in conflict with policies of the state or the Chinese Communist Party.[62]

Third, "teachers have the right to guide students in their studies and evaluate and help develop students' conduct and academic achievements."[63] This is the right to classroom management and student discipline. At the same time, teachers should respect the dignity of students and protect them from potential harms.[64] Accordingly, teachers are prohibited from discriminating against students and from using corporal punishment.[65]

Fourth, "teachers have the right to receive salaries and remunerations on schedule, to enjoy the welfare benefits prescribed by the State, and to take paid leave during the winter and summer vacations."[66] As mentioned earlier, laws require that teachers' salaries be higher than or at least equal to those of civil servants in the same region and that medical benefits available to teachers must be equivalent to those of public servants.[67]

Fifth, "teachers have the right to voice opinions and suggestions regarding teaching and learning, and the administration of schools and local educational agencies; and to participate in the democratic management of schools through assembly of teachers, staff and workers or through other forms."[68] This is about teachers' freedom of expression in relation to school management.

In this regard, the Constitution declares that Chinese citizens have a fundamental right to criticize government agencies and civil servants without being subject to retaliation.[69] In doing so, though, teachers are prohibited from fabricating or distorting facts.[70] The concept of being a "public figure," an element of the law of defamation in the United States, has not been established in Chinese law. In 2012, the Ministry of Education enacted the Provisions on the Faculty Representative Assembly of School, specifying the details on how faculty participate in school management through the assembly.

Sixth, "teachers have the right to continuing education or other forms of training."[71] Continuing education is both a right and a duty for teachers. The Regulation on the Continuing Education of Elementary and Secondary School Teachers (1999) mandates that elementary and secondary school teachers receive at least 120 hours of in-service training during their probationary period and at least 240 hours for every five years they retain their jobs as teachers. More recently, the Provisional Method on Periodical Registration of Elementary and Secondary School Teacher License (2013) requires 360 hours of continuing education or the equivalent as specified by the respective provisional education agency for a five-year license registration period.

Unions

Teachers have the right to join unions. In China, there is only one major union, the All-China Federation of Trade Unions (ACFTU).[72] Workplace-based union organizations[73] and regionally based union organizations, as well as professionally based union organizations,[74] are all supposed to be divisions of ACFTU. School-level union leaders are paid by their employers.[75]

Unions are supposed to represent and safeguard the interests of their members.[76] If school officials impinge on the legitimate interests of teachers, their unions can investigate[77] and request that officials discontinue the offending actions.[78] Union are also supposed to organize employees to participate in democratic decision making in their schools;[79] voice employees' concerns regarding salaries, workplace safety, employee insurance, and other benefits;[80] and sponsor and organize training, entertainment, and sporting activities in collaboration with their employers.[81] In private schools, unions can negotiate with school officials and sign a collective bargaining agreement on behalf of the employee.[82]

In China, civil servants,[83] judges,[84] public procurators,[85] and public security officers[86] are prohibited from participating in strikes.[87] The law is not explicit regarding whether other employees have the right to strike, but it imposes a duty on unions to negotiate with employers if work stoppages or slowdowns occur.[88]

Equal Protection

Insofar as school teaching, especially elementary school teaching, is primarily a female profession in China, gender equality is a particularly important issue. In China, women have a fundamental constitutional right to earn equal pay for equal work.[89] Employers are prohibited from dismissing female employees during their pregnancies, maternity leaves, and nursing periods.[90] Female employees can take maternity leave for ninety-eight days.[91] When their maternity leaves overlap with summer or winter breaks, female teachers can take extended leave for the overlapping periods.[92] On the other hand, to address the gender imbalance in faculty composition, some teacher education programs and provincial educational agencies have attempted to lower admission requirements for male applicants. This practice has been challenged as gender discrimination.

The last ten years have witnessed many equal protection challenges to teacher education admission and recruitment practices. Applicants have been successful in removing the height and body weight restriction as well as the discrimination against hepatitis B virus carriers. Still, some provinces still do not allow those who lost both upper limbs, those who lost both lower limbs, those whose two lower limbs have a difference in length of more than 5 cm, and those who have big scars on the face from applying for teacher licenses.[93] Such restrictions may have a discriminating impact on applicants with disabilities.

STUDENT RIGHTS

Equal Protection

Gender

Equal rights for women are a fundamental right in the Constitution.[94] The Education Law,[95] the Compulsory Education Law,[96] and the Law on the Protection of the Rights and Interests of Women[97] further specify that female students have equal rights in enrollment, placement, degree conferral, and overseas study. In the past, colleges and vocational schools were able to apply different admission requirements, in specified fields, to the male and female applicants. In recent years, such obvious discrimination has become less and less.

Insofar as sexual harassment is a serious threat to girls' opportunities to receive education, especially in rural areas, it is banned by the Law on the Protection of the Rights and Interests of Women.[98] In China, because institutional liability has not been established, harassers may be subjected to administrative and civil liabilities.[99] If the harassment amounts to molestation or rape, criminal liability also applies.

In response to a series of hideous incidents, in 2013 the Ministry of Education issued a policy on the prevention of sexual abuse of children jointly with the Ministry of Public Security and other official youth and women's organizations.[100] The policy calls for better education of teachers, students, and parents against sexual abuse. Further, the policy requires officials in local educational agencies to establish reporting systems for student sexual abuse.

Education of Minority Students

In addition to the Han ethnicity, there are fifty-five minority ethnicities in China.[101] According to the law, all ethnicities shall be equal[102] and citizens have equal educational opportunities regardless of their ethnicity.[103] Regional autonomy is practiced where ethnic minorities live in compact communities,[104] and education is one such area of self-governance.[105] The state subsidizes education in poor minority areas[106] and provides assistance for poor minority students to finish their studies.[107] In admission to higher education or specialized upper secondary schools, a form of affirmative action exists. Under these plans, bonus points are made available to minority students and special considerations can be given to applicants from ethnic-minority groups with very small populations.[108]

The Constitution recognizes that every minority group has the freedom to use and develop its own language.[109] However, the Education Law and the Law on Nation-wide Commonly-used Languages and Characters stipulate that standardized Chinese, or Mandarin, is the language of instruction to be used in schools.[110] The language policy for minorities used to be minority language instruction, if conditions allowed, with Chinese classes starting to be offered in elementary schools.[111]

In the amendment to the Education Law in 2015, the setup for bilingual education (*shuangyu jiaoyu*) was made explicit. The state has the responsibility to "facilitate and support" the implementation of bilingual education.[112] It should be noted that based on the wording of both the old and new laws that this offering of bilingual education is limited to "schools and other educational institutions dominated by ethnic minority students in ethnic autonomous areas." In other words, outside of the ethnic autonomous areas or in schools not dominated by minority students, bilingual education is not necessarily offered.

Education of Migrant Children

Migrant children are not a legal category for equal protection under the Constitution or the Education Law. Even so, the right to education of migrant children is an issue that cannot be overlooked in China. Migrant children are those who are originally from other places, mostly the countryside, but who live in the cities where their parents are currently working. Insofar as the right to attend neighborhood schools in China is directly conditioned on formal household registration, which for migrant families is fixed to their hometowns, migrant children do not have entitlements to public education in the cities where they currently live.

The amendment to the Compulsory Education Law in 2005 requires local governments to provide migrant children with "equal conditions for receiving compulsory education."[113] How to create such "equal conditions" is up to the provincial governments to decide. Some provincial governments set out a series of conditions and demand complicated paperwork.[114] As a result, many migrant children are kept out of free city public schools: some attend private schools in the cities where they live and some are sent by their parents back to their hometowns to receive public education.

The State Council issued a policy in 2012 addressing the opportunity of migrant students to receive post-compulsory education in the cities where they currently reside.[115] In the past, such migrant students, restricted by the household registration system, usually had to return to their hometowns to take the entrance examinations into upper-secondary schools or colleges. The 2012 policy urges each province to adopt its own rules to address this issue. As a result, many provinces, although still keeping public upper-secondary schools out of reach of the majority of migrant students, allow migrant students to be enrolled in local vocational schools.

Due Process

In compulsory education, schools are banned from expelling students.[116] The Law on the Protection of Minors also prohibits the capricious expulsion of minors from schools.[117] Besides expulsion, disciplinary actions for students in elementary and secondary education include warnings (*jinggao*), severe warnings (*yanzhong jinggao*), demerits on record (*jiguo*), and probation (*liuxiao chakan*). Yet national laws have not systematically articulated the conditions and procedures for student discipline in elementary and secondary education.

Due process protection was first upheld in a case from higher education involving a student. In *Tian Yong v. Beijing University of Science and Technology* (1999), a trial court in Beijing ruled that university officials violated the student's rights to notice and defense in the face of the negative action they took against him.[118] This judgment was soon printed in the official journal of the Supreme People's Court in 1999 and later became a "guiding case" after the case guidance system was established in 2010. The due process measures upheld in *Tian Yong* may have broad implications for elementary and secondary education.

Some provincial or local policies have made specified due process measures available to elementary and secondary school students within their jurisdictions. For example, the Department of Education of Shandong province requires elementary and secondary schools to have hearing systems in place.[119] A rule issued by the Education Bureau of Qingdao, a city in Shandong, specifies how to request hearings, who is allowed to participate, and the rights students have in such hearing processes.[120] It is also generally required that parents be notified of the disciplinary sanctions their children face.[121] Given the evolving nature of school law in China and the substantive attention that has been directed to due process, it may be expected that these due process protections will be provided to K–12 students nationwide in the future.

Search and Seizure

Search and seizure by school personnel is not unusual in Chinese schools, especially in less developed areas. Common instances include searches of students' dormitories and personal bags, as well as their diaries, mails, emails, and cell phone communications. From a legal perspective, freedom from unlawful search and privacy of correspondence are fundamental rights under the Constitution.[122] As an additional protection, the Law on the Protection of Minors[123] safeguards the correspondence privacy rights of minors.

As the consciousness of individual rights rises in China, the prevalence of traditional search and seizure may have dropped especially in developed areas. In the information age, though, the growth and use of technology may pose new challenges. The widespread installation of surveillance cameras in schools has raised some privacy concerns from parents and students. The regulation of students' cell phones is also controversial in some schools, a topic discussed in the section on emerging issues.

Freedom of Religion

As individual citizens, students have the constitutional right to "believe in, or not to believe in, any religion."[124] Students cannot be discriminated against due to their religious beliefs or lack thereof.[125] Yet it is not clear if and to what extent religious accommodations are provided in Chinese public schools, especially in those outside of autonomous ethnic areas. Given the separation of religion and the education system[126] and the restriction of group religious activities to registered places of worship,[127] religious groups do not have equal access to public schools. Even so, religious academies can be established if they meet specified conditions and obtain government approval.[128]

Special Education

The rights of students with disabilities are protected in the constitution,[129] educational laws,[130] and disability laws.[131] Persons with disabilities have equal rights to education.[132] For children with disabilities who have reached school age, educational and health care agencies at county levels should offer consulting on schooling options (*jiuxue zixun*), assessing the disabilities of children and offering placement opinions.[133]

Depending on the categories of disabilities and students' capabilities to cope with school life, three types of placement are available: *Suibanjiudu*, or attending regular classes within regular schools; attending special education classes within regular schools, child welfare institutions, or other organizations; and attending special education schools.[134]

Over time there has been more policy emphasis on placing students with disabilities in inclusive settings. Educators in regular schools have responsibilities to provide education to students who are "capable of receiving ordinary education" and to "offer convenience and aid" for their study.[135] If officials in regular schools refuse to enroll such students, they or their guardians may seek help from relevant authorities, which shall "order the school to admit the students."[136] In recent years, there has also a policy effort to require new construction for public purposed and state-administered tests barrier-free.[137]

EMERGING ISSUES

With the spread of technology, students' use of cell phones, tablets, and other mobile devices has become an issue that school administrators and teachers have to face. In China, few local educational agencies have policies regarding campus cell phone use. The regulation regarding cell phone use is usually at the school level. School cell phone policies can be put in three categories: institutional rules, written policies, and the soft approach.[138]

A survey of school teachers in Shenzhen, the industrial and commercial city adjacent to Hong Kong, reveals that significant differences exist between elementary, middle, and high school levels on the number of schools banning students' cell phone use, the forms of the policies, and the policy reinforcement strategies.[139] Policies in elementary and middle schools are more likely than high schools to call for bans of student cell phone use in schools. Reports of school teachers' confiscation and the following escalated teacher-student conflict often appear in the media. In some situations, teachers have thrown students' cell phones to the floor and in other more extreme instances, some school officials burned confiscated cell phones while making it into a ceremony for student education.

A variety of legal risks exist in schools that have enacted cell phone regulation policies and practices. Confiscation and even destruction of cell phones impinges on students' property rights. Probably because of this, officials in some schools choose to establish boxes for temporary holding cell phones in each classroom and use student volunteers to take charge of the boxes. Getting access to information on students' cell phones may also impinge students' rights to privacy. But generally, if school policies or teachers simply restrict or prohibits student use of cell phones in schools, a small proportion of parents may complain about the inconvenience, but few have brought legal challenges against these policies.

The regulation of cell phone use is a response to the impacts of new technology on schools. At the same time, bullying is an old issue that has been exacerbated in the information age when the Internet becomes both a site and a means for bullying video transmission.

In China, schools have the responsibilities for educating, managing, and protecting students. School officials can be liable if they are negligent in protecting students from dangers of which they know or should have known. In 2016, school bullying has become a focal issue of educational policy concern. The Ministry of Education is currently drafting a policy specifically addressing school bullying. Besides legal liabilities, the new policy will provide guidance on bullying prevention, education measures, and response procedures.

CONCLUSION AND DISCUSSION

The Education Law lays down the institutional foundations of elementary and secondary education in China. This chapter has examined legal issues related to school administration, faculty rights, and students' rights in China, illuminating the complex relationships between the state, schools, students, and faculty. The chapter has also explored emerging legal issues in contemporary China. This last section of the chapter fleshes out relationships that have helped shape the legal landscape of elementary and secondary education in China.

State and Local Relationships

On the one hand, China is not a federalist country. Article 3 of the Constitution (1982) stipulates that the central government has "unified leadership." The right to education is also a fundamental right of citizenship under the Constitution. As a result, the central government has the ultimate say on educational issues and its orders can be implemented in a top-down manner.

On the other hand, according to the Education Law,[140] elementary and secondary education is "administered by the local people's governments under the guidance of the State Council." In other words, the administration of elementary and secondary education is primarily a local issue. Because of regional disparity in economic development, some local governments cannot provide sufficient funding for elementary and secondary education, especially in the rural west. Around the turn of century, stories about poor rural school conditions or delayed salary payment for public school teachers often made the headlines. In such a context, the Compulsory Education Law was amended in 2006, establishing a school finance system with shared responsibilities[141] and intergovernment transfers.[142]

If this finance system is to ensure basic equity in educational provision in the whole of China, "giving full play to the initiative and enthusiasm of the local authorities" is also part of the constitutional principle governing the state-local relationship.[143] Some local governments in developed areas are trying to make non-compulsory upper-secondary education free. Other provincial or local rules provide students or faculty with more protection than the state mandates.

Laws, Administrative Rules, and Judicial Rulings

Legislative supremacy, rather than separation of powers, is the fundamental principle of state governance in China. The National People's Congress is "the highest organ of state power."[144] Select statutes, the narrowly defined laws—such as the Education Law, Compulsory Education, Vocational Law, Teachers Law, Law on the Promotion of Non-public Schools, and Law on the Protection of Minors—shape the foundation of the legal landscape of elementary and secondary education in China.

The vast majority of educational laws, broadly defined, come from the central and local administrations. The metaphor of an iceberg can be used to describe the shape and structure of education law in China. On the very top is the Constitution. Near the top are the above mentioned few statutes. The base part is constituted by many formally promulgated administrative regulations (*xingzheng fagui*) and administrative rules (*xingzheng guizhang*), such as the Regulation of Teacher Licenses, and Rules in Dealing with Student Injury and Accidents.

A huge part of the law is also below the sea level in the form of central or local education policies. Strictly speaking, such policies are not official sources of law in China. However, detailed regulations and policy innovations often come from this last level. The direction of policy innovation may be bottom-up or top-down in China. Some successful policies are later incorporated into administrative rules and regulations, and statutes. In delineating the legal landscape of elementary and secondary education in China, this chapter therefore has included laws from all these levels.

Judicial rulings have become an important force in shaping the landscape of elementary and secondary education law. Students and their legal guardians are increasingly using the judiciary to claim their rights, especially on issues relevant to equal protection, due process, and information freedom. Although many have failed, some cases have triggered subsequent policy and legislative changes. In other words, there are some interbranch interactions between the judiciary, the administration, and the legislation.

Student/Faculty, School, and Government Relationships

The legal landscape of elementary and secondary education is essentially a result of the intricate relationship between and among the state, students and their parents, and school officials. Compulsory education, the foundational concept in contemporary elementary and secondary education, is a perfect example.

On the one hand, the state mandates students' enrollment in school for the purposes of building human capital and citizenship. On the other hand, in return for compulsory enrollment, the state has responsibilities to establish and fund schools. This results in a series of institutional issues, including the establishment of public schools, the development of school administration systems, and public expenditure for education. In addition, because school attendance is mandatory, officials in schools offering compulsory education are prohibited from expelling students. Given their public nature, moreover, schools are required by the state to treat students equally, protect their rights and interests, and provide due process measures for student discipline.

The role of faculty enters the configuration of the legal landscape as instruction providers to students and as school employees. As instruction providers, teachers have the rights, and responsibilities in many instances, to choose instructional methods, to conduct relevant research, to discipline students, and to receive continuing education. As school employees, teachers have the right to receive salaries, benefits and paid leaves, and to participate in school governance. In order to ensure the quality of teaching and the justice of interactions with their students, the state imposes teacher licensure requirements along with teacher ethics standards. To further safeguard their rights of teachers as school employees, the state protects their rights to unionize and to equal protection.

One special feature in this legal landscape in China is the legal status of school. Public schools are not directly part of the state, but a type of public enterprises (*shiye danwei*). Both private and public relationships exist between schools and students. The private or civil relationship is fairly clear. The in locos parentis principle has been rejected. The school has a responsibility to educate and manage students. School officials are liable for student injuries only when they are negligent. In comparison, grievances related to student discipline or the right to equal protection emerge out of public relationships.

The Chinese judicial system operates in three distinctive divisions: criminal, civil, and administrative. When public schools are defined as public enterprises rather than part of the state, the administrative division of the courts sometimes refuses to hear cases, an outcome which leaves students' rights unprotected while hindering the dynamic interplays between the courts, administrations/legislation, and social change. In the future, Chinese students have to be provided clearly with the right to seek judicial remedy in student discipline or equal protection disputes.

NOTES

1. Ministry of Education, Education Statistics of 2014.

2. *Tian Yong v. Beijing University of Science and Technology* (1999); *He Xiaoqiang v. Huazhong University of Science and Technology* (2008).

3. Art. 46.

4. Education Law, art. 19 (1995, amended 2015). Compulsory Education Law, art.11 (1986, amended 2006). In some areas with insufficient conditions, the school enrollment age can be postponed to seven. The enrollment age and the length of compulsory schooling can be relaxed for students with special physical needs.

5. Education Law, art. 19 (1995, amended 2015).

6. Compulsory Education Law, art. 14 (1986, amended 2006). Law on Protection of Minors, art. 38 (1991, amended 2006) (PRC). State Council, Regulations on Prohibition against Child Labor (2002) (PRC). Child labor is defined as minors of less than sixteen years of age. The majority age in China is eighteen. If an employer hires a minor under eighteen years old, it is prohibited to assign the employee to a dangerous position.

7. Compulsory Education Law, art. 58 (1986, amended 2006).

8. Xiaoming Sheng, *Learning with Mothers: A Study of Home Schooling in China* (Rotterdam, The Netherlands: Sense Publishers, 2014).

9. Zaijia Shangxue Lianmeng [Homeschooling Liaison]. http://chinahomeschooling.com/portal.php.

10. Compulsory Education Law, art. 2 (1986, amended 2006).

11. Compulsory Education Law, art. 44, 46 (1986, amended 2006).

12. Education Law, art. 55 (1995, amended 2015).

13. Education Law, art. 56 (1995, amended 2015).

14. For example, the city government of Zhengzhou (in Henan Province), zhengzhoushi xueqian jiaoyuquan fafang guanli zanxing banfa [Provisional Measures on the Issuance of Preschool Education Vouchers] (2011).

15. The city government of Zhongwei (in the Ningxia Hui Autonomous Region), zhongweishi zhiye jiaoyuquan fafang guanli banfa (shixing) [The Provisional Measures on the Issuance of Vocational Education Vouchers] (2014).

16. The city government of Huzhou (in the Zhejiang Province), guanyu zhuanfa shi jiaoyuju deng bumen guanyu zai quanshi zhongxiaoxue shishi pinkun xuesheng zhuxue jiaoyuquan zhidu de tongzhi [Forwarding the Notice from the Education Bureau on Implementing Special Aid Vouchers for Students with Financial Difficulties in Elementary and Secondary Schools] (2003).

17. For the state policy on purchasing private service, please see the General Office of the State Council, guanyu zhengfu xiang shehui liliang goumai fuwu de zhidao yijian [Guidance on Governments' Purchase of Private Service] (2013).

18. Education Law, art. 15 (1995, amended 2015). Please note that the city level is higher than the county level in China. Each city usually comprises of a number of counties.

19. Education Law, art. 14 (1995, amended 2015).

20. Compulsory Education Law, art. 7 (1986, amended 2006).

21. Vocational Education Law, art. 12 (1996).

22. Vocational Education Law, art. 16 (1996).

23. Ministry of Finance, Ministry of Education, and Ministry of Human Resources and Social Security, zhongdeng zhiye xuexiao guojia zhuxuejin guanli banfa [Measures on State Student Aids for Secondary Vocational Schools] (2013).

24. Law on the Promotion of Non-Public Schools, art. 2 (2002); Education Law, art. 26 (1995, amended 2015).

25. Law on the Promotion of Non-Public Schools, art. 5 (2002).

26. Law on the Promotion of Non-Public Schools, art. 28 (2002).

27. Law on the Promotion of Non-Public Schools, art. 4 (2002).

28. Law on the Promotion of Non-Public Schools, art. 41 (2002); Implementation Methods for the Law on the Promotion of Non-Public Schools, art. 4 (2002).

29. Law on the Promotion of Non-Public Schools, art. 40 (2002).

30. Education Law, art. 25 (1995); Law on the Promotion of Non-Public Schools, art. 3 (2002). Some for-profit after-school tutoring "schools" are registered as business organizations, not as officially recognized schools.

31. Law on the Promotion of Non-Public Schools, art. 51 (2002). For specific calculation of "reasonable return" and its withdrawing procedures, please see State Council, minban jiaoyu cujinfa shishi tiaoli [Regulation on the Implementation of the Law on the Promotion of Non-public Schools], art. 37–47 (2002). Drawing attention to the profit-making behaviors in private colleges and universities, Yan and Lin characterized private higher education in China as "commercial civil society." See Fengqiao Yan and Jing Lin, *Commercial civil society: A perspective on private higher education in China*, 5 Frontiers of Education in China 558 (2010).

32. State Council, minban jiaoyu cujinfa shishi tiaoli [Implementation Methods for the Law on the Promotion of Non-Public Schools], art. 38 (2002).

33. Commission of Education, guanyu kaiban waiji renyuan zinv xuexiao de zanxing banfa [Tentative Measures for Administration on Establishment of Schools for Children of Foreign Personnel], art. 18 (1995). The Commission of Education is changed to Ministry of Education in 1998.

34. Ibid., art. 6, 8, 9, 16, 17. The approval authority originally resided in the Ministry of Education and moved to the provincial educational agency in 2012. Ministry of Education, guanyu zuohao waiji renyuan zinv xuexiao youguan gongzuo de yijian [Opinions on the Work related to the School for Children of Foreign Personnel] (2015).

35. It does not mean that children with foreign passports can only attend these two types of schools. They can attend the third type of schools as well as some rectified public and private schools.

36. State Council, zhongwai hezuo banxue tiaoli [Regulations on Chinese-foreign Cooperative Education], art. 2 (2003).

37. Ibid., art. 30, 31.

38. Ibid., art. 6.

39. For example, Beijing Huijia Private School. http://www.huijia.edu.cn/sc.

40. Xuesheng shanghai shigu chuli banfa [Rules in Dealing with Student Injury Accidents] art. 7 (2002).

41. Tort Law, art. 38, 39 (2009).

42. Tort Law, art. 39 (2009).

43. Tort Law, art. 40 (2009).

44. Teachers Law, art. 3 (1993, amended 2009).

45. Teachers Law, art. 10 (1993, amended 2009); State Council, jiaoshi zige tiaoli [A Regulation on Teacher Licensure], art. 2 (1995).

46. Ministry of Education, zhongxiaoxue jiaoshi zige kaoshi zanxing banfa [Temporary Method on the Licensure Test for Elementary and Secondary School Teachers], art. 4, 5, 18 (2013). Please note that the *Teachers Law* (1993) does allow applicants who have met the educational level requirements to be exempted from taking the licensure test. Please see Teachers Law, art. 13 (1993). The new Ministry of Education has made this exemption void. In implementation, taking the national licensure test is now a necessary step toward obtaining a teacher license.

47. Ministry of Education, zhongxiaoxue jiaoshi zige kaoshi zanxing banfa [Temporary Method on the Licensure Test for Elementary and Secondary School Teachers], art. 6 (2013). Article 11 of the Teachers Law specifies the minimum educational level requirements for obtaining a teacher licensure, which is fairly low and outdated. For example, to teach in an elementary school, the applicant only need to have graduated from a normal school. In the higher education massification process over the past twenty years, most normal schools have already escalated into teacher colleges offering associate degrees. It is expected that this provision will be amended in the near future.

48. Teachers Law, art. 13 (1993, amended 2009). Ministry of Education, zhongxiaoxue jiaoshi zige kaoshi zanxing banfa [Temporary Method on the Licensure Test for Elementary and Secondary School Teachers], art. 18 (2013).

49. Temporary Method on the Licensure Test for Elementary and Secondary School Teachers, art. 5 (2013).

50. Labor Contract Law, art. 2, 96 (2007, amended 2012).

51. Some selective higher education institutions are currently experimenting with a tenure system. But it is more of a kind of institutional innovation. It has not been recognized and incorporated into laws. On paperwork, tenured faculty members still need to sign a contract with the university, with the term of contract specified as permanent. The base of their employment relationship is still the contract. If there is a dispute, the dispute is still classified as a contract dispute.

52. Art. 14.

53. In China, universal mandatory retirement age exists. For public school teachers, the mandatory retirement age is sixty for the male and fifty-five for the female.

54. State Council, Shiye danwei renshi guanli tiaoli [Regulation on Personnel Management in Public Enterprises], art. 15.

55. Ministry of Education, Zhongxiaoxue jiaoshi weifan zhiye daode xingwei chuli banfa [The Disciplinary Measures on Elementary and Secondary School Teachers for Violating Professional Ethics], art. 4 (2014); Teachers Law, art. 37 (1993, amended 2009). For the professional norm on the positive side, please see Ministry of Education, Zhongxiaoxue jiaoshi zhiye daode guifan [Professional Ethics Norms for Elementary and Secondary School Teachers] (amended 2008); Teachers Law, art. 8 (1993, amended 2009).

56. Ministry of Education, Zhongxiaoxue jiaoshi weifan zhiye daode xingwei chuli banfa [The Disciplinary Measures on Elementary and Secondary School Teachers for Violating Professional Ethics], art. 7, 9 (2014); Teachers Law, art. 3, 37 (1993, amended 2009).

57. Ministry of Education, Zhongxiaoxue jiaoshi weifan zhiye daode xingwei chuli banfa [The Disciplinary Measures on Elementary and Secondary School Teachers for Violating Professional Ethics], art. 2 (2014).

58. Ministry of Education, Zhongxiaoxue jiaoshi weifan zhiye daode xingwei chuli banfa [The Disciplinary Measures on Elementary and Secondary School Teachers for Violating Professional Ethics], art. 5 (2014).

59. Ministry of Education, Zhongxiaoxue jiaoshi weifan zhiye daode xingwei chuli banfa [The Disciplinary Measures on Elementary and Secondary School Teachers for Violating Professional Ethics], art. 10 (2014); Teachers Law, art. 39 (1993, amended 2009).

60. The Teachers Law, art. 7 (1993, amended 2009).

61. The Teachers Law, art. 7 (1993, amended 2009).

62. Ministry of Education, Zhongxiaoxue jiaoshi weifan zhiye daode xingwei chuli banfa [The Disciplinary Measures on Elementary and Secondary School Teachers for Violating Professional Ethics], art. 4 (2014).

63. The Teachers Law, art. 7 (1993, amended 2009).

64. Ibid., art. 8.

65. Compulsory Education Law, art. 29 (1986, amended 2006). See also Ministry of Education, Zhongxiaoxue jiaoshi weifan zhiye daode xingwei chuli banfa [The Disciplinary Measures on Elementary and Secondary School Teachers for Violating Professional Ethics], art. 4 (2014).

66. The Teachers Law, art. 7 (1993).

67. Ibid., art. 25, 29, 28.

68. Ibid., art. 7.

69. Constitution, art. 41 (1982). See also the Teachers Law, art. 36 (1993, amended 2009).

70. Constitution, art. 41 (1982); General Principles of the Civil Law, art. 101 (1986).

71. The Teachers Law, art. 7 (1993, amended 2009).

72. The Trade Union Law, art. 2, 10 (1992, amended 2009). The official website is http://www.acftu.org/.

73. They do not necessarily have an independent legal status. The Trade Union Law, art. 14 (1992, amended 2009).

74. Unions federation in the county or above level can have an independent legal status, but they are still a subdivision of the ACFTU. The Trade Union Law, art. 14 (1992, amended 2009).

75. The Trade Union Law, art. 40, 41 (1992, amended 2009).

76. The Trade Union Law, art. 2 (1992). It shall be noted that the union is not supposed to only represent the interests of union members. The word "employees" is used throughout the *Trade Union Law* when describing unions' goals and activities, while the word "members" is only associated with internal structure of unions. Nonunion members do not need to pay a fee for the union's representation.

77. Ibid., art. 25.

78. Ibid., art. 22.

79. Ibid., art. 5, 6, 19.

80. Ibid., art. 30, 38.

81. Ibid., art. 31.

82. Ibid., art. 20. All China Federation of Trade Union and Ministry of Education, zai shehui liliang juban de xuexiao jianli gonghui zuzhi de yijian [Opinions on Establishing Trade Union Branches in Private Schools] (2002). In contrast, the "base" teacher salary in public schools is set by standard government policies.

83. Civil Servant Law, art. 53 (2005).

84. Judges Law, art. 32 (1995, amended 2001).

85. Public Procurators Law, art. 35 (1995, amended 2001).

86. People's Police Law, art. 22 (1995, amended 2012).

87. Under both the 1975 and the 1978 amendments to the Constitution (1954), citizens have a right to strike. This provision was dropped in the Constitution of 1982.

88. The Trade Union Law, art. 27 (1992).

89. Constitution, art. 48 (1982).

90. Law on the Protection of the Rights and Interests of Women, art. 27 (1992, amended 2005); Labor Law, art. 29 (1994); State Council, nv zhigong laodong baohu tebie guiding [Special rules on the Labor Protection of Female Employees], art. 5 (2012).

91. State Council, nv zhigong laodong baohu tebie guiding [Special rules on the Labor Protection of Female Employees], art. 7 (2012). Article 62 of the Labor Law (1994) stipulates that maternity leave for the female is at least ninety days.

92. Education Commission, guanyu nv jiaoshi chanjia youguan wenti de fuhan [A Reply on Maternal Leaves for Female Teachers] (1992).

93. Department of Education of Jiangxi Province, guanyu xiuding "Jiangxi sheng shenbao rending jiaoshi zige renyuan tijian banfa" (shixing) de tongzhi [A Notice on Revising the Provisional Physical Examination Methods for Teacher Licensure Application] (2010).

94. Art. 48 (1982).

95. Art. 36 (1995, amended 2015).

96. Art. 4 (1986, amended 2006).

97. Art. 15-21 (1992, amended 2005).

98. Art. 40 (1992, amended 2005).

99. Ibid., art. 58.

100. Ministry of Education, Ministry of Public Security, Central Committee of the Chinese Communist Youth League, and the All-China Women's Federation, Guanyu zuohao yufang shaonian ertong zaoshou xingqin gongzuo de yijian [Opinions on the Effective Prevention of Sexual Abuse of Juvenile and Children] (2013).

101. Some scholars maintain that Chinese law does not provide a definition of "minority" and that these fifty-five recognized groups are "minority nationalities" rather than "minorities." Some nationalities are not recognized due to their small population. See Bai Guimei, "The International Covenant on Civil and Political Rights and the Chinese Law on the Protection of the Rights of Minority Nationalities," 3 Chinese J. I. L. 468 (2004).

102. Constitution, art. 4 (1982).

103. The Education Law, art. 46 (1995).

104. Constitution, art. 4 (1982).

105. Constitution, art. 119 (1982). Law on the Regional National Autonomy, art. 36, 37 (1984, amended 2001).

106. Education Law, art. 10 (1995); Law on the Regional National Autonomy, art. 37, § 2 (1984).

107. Law on the Regional National Autonomy, art. 71 (1984).

108. Law on the Regional National Autonomy, art. 71 (1984).

109. Constitution, art. 4 (1982); see also Law on the Nation-wide Commonly-used Languages and Characters, art. 8 (2000).

110. Education Law, art. 12 (1995, amended 2015). Law on the Nation-wide Commonly-used Languages and Characters, art. 10, (2000).

111. Law on the Regional National Autonomy, art. 37 (1984, amended 2001) (PRC).

112. Education Law, art. 12 (1995, amended 2015).

113. Ibid., Art. 12.

114. For example, parents need to have worked and paid social security tax for several years in their city of residence. This is difficult for many migrant families to achieve, in part because migrant workers frequently move and change jobs, and in part because some employers do not sign a formal contract with migrant workers and avoid social security tax.

115. General Office of the State Council, guanyu zhuanfa jiaoyu deng bumen zuohao jincheng wugong renyuan suiqian zinv jieshou yiwu jiaoyu hou zai dangdi canjia shengxue kaoshi gongzuo yijian de tongzhi [A Notice on Forwarding the Working Opinions on Allowing Children of Migrant Population to Receive Post-Compulsory Education in Their Place of Residence] (2012).

116. Compulsory Education Law, art. 27 (1986, amended 2006).

117. The Law on the Protection of Minors, art. 18 (1991, amended 2012).

118. An English translation of this decision is available at *Chinese Education and Society*, vol. 39, iss. 3, 59–69 (2006).

119. Department of Education of Shandong Province, Shandong sheng putong zhongxiaoxue xueji guanli guiding (shixing) [Regulation on Student Record Management in General Elementary and Secondary Schools in Shandong Province (in trial)], art. 30 (2007).

120. Education Bureau of Qingdao, Zhongxiaoxue chufen zanxing guiding [Provisional Regulation on Student Discipline in Elementary and Secondary Schools], art. 13 (2002).

121. Commission of Education, Zhongxiaoxue deyu gongzuo guicheng [Regulation on Moral Education in Elementary and Secondary School], art. 27 (1998). See also, for example, Regulation on Student Record Management in Elementary and Secondary Schools in Shanghai, art. 47 (2006); Regulation on Student Record Management in General Elementary and Secondary Schools in Shandong Province (in trial), art. 30 (2007).

122. Constitution, art. 37, 40 (1982).

123. The Law on the Protection of Minors, art. 39 (1991, amended 2012).

124. Constitution, art. 36 (1982).

125. In addition to the Constitution, see also Law on Regional National Autonomy, art. 11 (1984, amended 2001). State Council, Zongjiao shiwu tiaoli [Regulation on Religious Affairs], art. 2 (2004).

126. Constitution, art. 36 (1982). See also Law on Regional National Autonomy, art. 11 (1984, amended 2001). Education Law, art. 8 (1995, amended 2005).

127. Regulation on Religious Affairs, art. 12 (2004).

128. Regulation on Religious Affairs, art. 8, 9 (2004).

129. Art. 45, § 3 (1982).

130. Compulsory Education Law (1986, amended 2006), Education Law (1995, amended 2015).

131. The Law on the Protection of Persons with Disabilities (1991, amended 2008), Regulations on the Education of Persons with Disabilities (1994, amended 2011).

132. Regulations on the Education of Persons with Disabilities, art. 21 (1994, amended 2011).

133. Regulation on the Education of Persons with Disabilities, art. 16 (1994, amended 2011).

134. The Law on the Protection of Persons with Disabilities, art. 23, 25, 26 (1991, amended 2008); Regulation on the Education of Persons with Disabilities, art. 17 (1994, amended 2011).

135. The Law on the Protection of Persons with Disabilities, art. 25 (1991, amended 2008); Compulsory Education Law, art. 19 (1986, amended 2006); Education Law, art. 38 (1995, amended 2015).

136. The Law on the Protection of Persons with Disabilities, art. 25 (1991, amended 2008).

137. The Law on the Protection of Persons with Disabilities, art. 52–58 (1991, amended 2008); State Council, wu zhang'ai huanjing jianshe tiaoli [Regulation on the Construction of Barrier-Free Environments] (2012).
138. AZAD I. ALI, et al., *Dealing with the distractions of cell phone misuse/use in the classroom—a case example*, 10 Competition Forum (2012).
139. Q. F. GAO, et al., *To ban or not to ban: Differences in mobile phone policies at elementary, middle, and high schools*, 38 Computers in Human Behavior (2014).
140. Art. 14.
141. Art. 44.
142. Art. 46.
143. Constitution, art. 3 (1982).
144. Constitution, art. 57 (1982).

Chapter Two

Israel

Dan Gibton

INTRODUCTION

The rights of students and the right to education were not part of education law in Israel's first five decades of legal tradition even though the courts often mentioned them explicitly, directly, or inadvertently. In 1995, the Supreme Court of Israel, in its role as a High Court of Justice, handed down a landmark ruling.[1] After detailed review and scrutiny of constitutional, administrative, educational, and case law, the Court found that the right to education is not embedded in Israeli law as a constitutional right, a social right, or a constitutional interest.[2]

Following the Supreme Court's decision, in 2000, Israel's parliament, the Knesset, accepted a bill that enacted the Student's Rights Act 2000, part of an overall thrust toward establishing students' rights in Israel's K–12 education. This chapter thus reviews the state of students' rights in Israel's schools, with attention to legislation, court rulings, government commissions, politics, pedagogy, along with problems and prospects as well as a look at the rights of teachers; in the process, the chapter also examines the features of the various types of schools in Israel and how they are funded.

LEGAL SYSTEM

Founded in 1948, Israel is a parliamentary democracy. The legal system in Israel was influenced by the principle of legal continuity, especially in its early years, from the Ottoman and English legal systems because Palestine was previously part of the Ottoman Empire and later, after World War I, a British mandate. Israel does not have a formal written constitution and therefore legally, the Knesset, its parliament, the legislator of the law of the land, votes in the executive branch—Israel's Prime Minister and government.

The judiciary, consisting of magistrate, district, and supreme courts, is totally independent. Judges are appointed by a special committee including the Secretary of Justice augmented by members of the Knesset, Supreme Court justices, and members of the Bar. The attorney general and chief legal advisor in the system presents legal directives to the government. Israel's supreme court has, from its early days, laid and strengthened the foundations of the nation's constitutional and administrative laws, forged the borders of human rights and citizenship, and created its case law by introducing a right's discourse that was influenced at first by British law and later by American Supreme Court rulings as well.

In addition to the criminal and civil three-tiered court system, a parallel systems exists in family law (in separate religious courts for Jews and Muslims with decisions being made according to religious laws of those faiths), Labor courts, and military tribunals. All of these judicial bodies are procedurally and rights-discourse subordinate to the Supreme Court of Israel.

Israel's elected parliament, the Knesset, enacts primary and secondary legislation. Attempts to establish a written constitution when Israel was founded failed mainly due to severe discrepancies on possible separation of "church (or synagogue) and state." Israel's Declaration of Independence identifies the nation as "Jewish and Democratic." Moreover, although the Declaration assures equality for all groups in Israel this dual, and often incongruous, definition between "Jewish" and "Democratic" has been an endless source for debates and arguments in the Knesset, the media, and, of course, in the courts on issues of citizenship for new immigrants, family law, and streams and content of public education.

Following Israel's failure to write a formal constitution, the Knesset accepted various enactments titled *Basic Laws*. These laws deal with basic rights issues such as "Human Dignity and Liberties," "Freedom of Occupation," the operation of the Knesset, the government, the presidency, the courts, the army, and the budget. These basic laws were envisioned as parts of an ongoing constitutional construction process, but to this day do not deal with issues of citizenship for non-Jews, family law, freedom of expression, and separation of "church (or synagogue) and state"—issues dealt with regularly by the Supreme Court. Therefore the Basic Laws have not fulfilled, as of yet, the inspiration to create a written constitution. As Harris et al. explained, "rights received much more attention than institutions."[3]

It is important to note that Israeli law only recognized the right to education formally only in 2000. Even so, various education laws passed in the early years of Israel's independence established and secured K–12 education, including religious education for Jews and education in Arabic for Palestinian-Israelis. A large body of case law by the Supreme Court and district courts fortified and further developed these rights. In addition to the Supreme Court, district courts have the power to try human rights petitions. This authority has increased the volume of such judicial reviews that benefited education case law considerably are presented in this chapter.

CONCEPTUAL FRAMEWORK: THE CONFLICT OF STUDENTS' RIGHTS IN EDUCATION

The International Convention on the Rights of the Child (UNCRC, UN 1989, ratified by Israel in 1991), has augmented alertness toward pupils' rights.[4] The most important of these rights are equality and protection from discrimination (Article 2), protection of the child's interests (Article 3), the right to life, survival, and development (Article 6), and the right to express views and opinions (Article 12). Articles 28–30 deal specifically with rights in education and schooling.

Addressing the rights of children is a relatively new topic in the discourse of rights.[5] Children are perhaps the last group that can be, sadly, legally and socially discriminated against, the common excuses being "age," "insufficient development or judgment," and similar general statements, often not necessarily corroborated with specific psychological, or moral, justifications. Children are often viewed as "half baked" or incomplete adults, with educators especially not always considering childhood an authentic stage of life in which the young have perhaps a unique, but legitimate, worldview that should be listened to and respected, particularly by those adults responsible for the formal education of the young.[6] In Freeman's words, "The emphasis shifted from protection to autonomy, from nurturance to self-determination, from welfare to justice."[7]Thus,

> Key issues relating to rights and education, such as multi-professional working, accessing the curriculum, taking account of children's and young people's voices, and educating for rights as part of a social justice agenda.[8]

Challenging the Rawlsian[9] contractual or mutual idea of justice, Nussbaum defines Human Capabilities, some of which are exceptionally relevant to education:

> Being able to use one's mind in ways protected by guarantees of freedom of expression with respect to both political and artistic speech, and freedom of religion exercise.
> Being able to form a conception of the good and to engage in critical reflection about the planning of one's life.
> Being able to live with and towards others . . . to engage in various forms of social interaction; . . . This entails nondiscrimination on the basis of race, sex, sexual orientation, ethnicity, caste, religion, national origin.

> Being able to participate effectively in political choices that govern one's life.[10]

Brighouse's[11] critique of the "human capital theory approach" that attempts to grant everybody general benefits as the result of training pupils to be productive workers discusses this foundation. Even so, he offers an alternate, wider set of goals in striving for autonomy and a flourishing life for all. Rejecting the Rawlsian theory of mutuality has significant implications for the rights of students, as the close quarters and small groups of schools and classrooms, create tensions around the distribution of goods far greater than, for example, on municipal or national levels.

There are three subgroups of pupil's rights in schools:[12] the right to education that is about acquiring knowledge and creating opportunities for further education; the rights in education which concern pupils' rights as "citizens" of their schools; and rights through education which are about the "apprenticeship"[13]—the status of students as future participating citizens of a democratic society. These three subgroups of rights carry the seeds of conflict. For instance: the right to education of a violent or disturbing pupil might clash with those of other students, while the rights in education and through education might cause disruption in school officials' attempt to allow freedom of expression or religion.[14]

> However, at the same time, a direct address of the United Nations Convention on the Rights of the Child within UK policy has been difficult to identify. Instead, children's rights have been taken forward in indirect ways as part of an outcomes-driven political agenda.[15]

Teachers, who nurture and develop a welcomed "ethic of care"[16] do not always see childhood as authentic, which often mandates that students should be recognized as "citizens" and not as "subjects" of their schools. The fact that the discourse of student rights[17] emerged from an adversarial situation in which rights protect citizens from the abuse of power by rulers, sovereigns, and governments does not contribute to the acceptance of pupils' rights in schools because they carry a hidden agenda that rights are there to protect students from their teachers.

Moreover, finally, as teachers themselves are often a disenfranchised group of professionals whose status is threatened and criticized,[18] the discourse on rights may be seen as a further infringement on their positions and authority.

Nevertheless, a sufficient body of knowledge demonstrates that schools are places where the rights of children are insufficiently guarded. Racism, discrimination, marginalization, and infringements on privacy are common in schools.[19] The concept of guarding and nurturing rights in and through education, in addition to the duty to promote the right *to* education, also require a rights discourse in everyday school life and a constitutional approach to the treatment of students.

Conceptual Legal and Sociopolitical Background: Student Rights 1953–2000

Israel is an immigrant multicultural liberal democracy involved in a serious military dispute about land and recognition, and, at the same time, is under worldwide pressure over its problematic control of Palestinian territories and people. The tension from this conflict casts a shadow on issues of the right to education, as will be seen; yet this is not the only conflict.

Twenty-one percent of Israeli citizens are Arab-Palestinians who can be considered as an indigenous nation as well as a distinctive ethnic and religious minority. Arab-Palestinians suffer from ongoing discrimination in funds and in degrees of autonomy in curriculum planning, especially in teaching their narrative on the political situation, although there are schools in which Arabic is taught throughout K–12 academic years.[20] Further tensions in Israel's society and education system include socioeconomic status (SES)-based gaps, including in education, between the financial and cultural centers in big cities and immigrant towns on the periphery. Further, there is still age-old tension between Sephardi and Ashkenazi Jews.

The core of educational legislation in Israel consists of the National Education Act of 1953;[21] the Compulsory Learning Act of 1949, under which school attendance is mandatory from age five to sixteen and free through the age of eighteen;[22] the School Supervision Act of 1969;[23] and, finally, the Special Education Act of 1988.[24] Together, these laws set the bases of Israel's educational system. Yet these laws do not include any per se rights discourse, although they provide K–12 compulsory, government-financed education, and the government's obligation to provide five types or streams of schools, plus the possibility of homeschooling, for every Israeli citizen.

One stream is the "National-Formal," that includes secular, government-commissioned and -delivered education, comprising some 60 percent of the system. This stream also includes a second substream of schools that teach in Arabic to Israeli-Palestinian citizens. The third stream, "National-Religious," provides Jewish modern-orthodox education is also fully maintained. The fourth stream, Jewish "ultra-orthodox" schools, also known as "Haredi," receive between full government maintenance and 55 percent of the basic government maintenance but are partially exempt from the National Curriculum. The fifth stream, marginal in size, is homeschooling that currently includes only a tiny fraction of the population.

In terms of commission of the system and provision of education services, schools from the first to fourth streams include both government or local authority–owned and –operated schools on the one hand, and schools owned and operated by private and semi-private entities, in the third and fourth sectors, chains, federations, and stand-alone schools. The overall proportion between government-commissioned and -delivered education and non-government schools is approximately 65 to 35 percent.

Most of the schools, but for a small group of Jewish ultra-orthodox schools, that are exempt from the legal requirements of the National Education Act teach adapted and ministry-authorized versions of the mandatory National Curriculum. These versions of the curricula include Islamic studies and Arabic for Palestinian-Israeli schools plus enhanced religious education for Jewish-religious schools.

Article Two of the National Education Act, 1953, and its subheading "Goals of National Education," identify the goals of national education. In Israel, national education is committed to educating students to love mankind, love their nation, and respect their culture and language; abide to Israel's principles as a Jewish-democratic state, and respect human rights, basic freedoms and democratic values, uphold the law, and respect other's culture and opinions.

In terms of the right to education, National Education is committed to the personality development of girls and boys. Other goals include the development of students' personal gifts and creativity so they can lead meaningful lives of quality; expanding students' knowledge of science and the human heritage of achievement; strengthening students critical thought while encouraging their curiosity, independent thought, and initiative; and inspiring students' involvement in society. Further goals include teaching students responsibility while honoring the environment as they also learn the culture, history, and language of the Arab minority and of other groups within Israel's society in recognizing the equal rights of all of Israel's citizens.

At the same time, Article 11 of the National Education Act allocates power to the Secretary of State for Education to grant formal recognition to the non-state schools, to impose and implement the National Curriculum, to define their governance arrangements, and to decree the government's financial support to the extent decided by the Secretary. Article 11, intended to allow minimal freedom for a residual tier of non-state schools, opened the door to a growing sector, which, after more than sixty-five years, includes over one quarter of Israel's schools and students.[25]

The "Recognized Non-Formal Schools" operating under Article 11 include over fifteen types of schools: secular and religious, Jewish and Arab, Muslim and Christian, vocational and academic. Among these schools are those belonging to the Green, or Eco-Friendly, movement while others represent progressive education including democratic and anthroposophical schools, some others focus on natural sciences, the arts, and an array of other contextual or pedagogical ideas. Many of these schools are organized and operated by nongovernmental Organizations (NGOs), and/or other associations, or were initiated by individuals or groups of parents. Although these schools receive generous government support, most of them supplement their budgets with private funds, gathered from parents, often creating de facto systems of segregation on financial grounds, on both the primary and secondary levels.

Discrimination, Segregation, and the Right to Education

During the 1970s, a comprehensive reform movement influenced by the post-*Brown* school desegregation era in the United States implemented mandatory integration in schools.[26] This integration was first, between Ashkenazi and Sephardi Jewish students, and later on, between high- and low-SES Israeli-Palestinians. Despite the worldwide interest in desegregation in the United States, Israel and the United States are the only two countries that attempted some form of mandatory integration via compulsory busing, strict attendance boundaries, and ethnic/racial balancing policy.

As with other school reforms in Israel, integration did not originate through primary legislation, but was supported fiercely by the Supreme Court of Israel for over two decades.[27] Integration reform received moderate resistance from both low-SES groups that saw it as forced streaming and Western enculturation, and high-SES groups that viewed it as "equaling down."

Despite the resistance, integration continues to be implemented throughout Israel. Still, integration was strongest for about two decades, 1970–1990. Although the results and implications of mandatory integration are part of public and educational debate to this day, in terms of the right to education this reform has had a dramatic positive effect, boosting accessibility to secondary, further, and higher education.

From a legal point of view, while the 1953 Act links the compliance of officials in Recognized Non-Formal Schools with government policy, and especially the National Curriculum, to public funding, in practice, enforcement by the Ministry of Education was loose. Large numbers of the "Recognized Non-Formal" schools became so due to coalition agreements with political parties, as part of attempts to harness their support to multiparty cabinets.

Gradually, and without any formal decision or structured schools reform, this group, or rather groups of schools, weakened control over public education while creating a heated discussion on the quality and character of public education and the right to education. Even now, this group poses serious threats to rights of equity, equality, and choice in education.[28] Court cases, a trickle at first that has become a steady flow, allowed the allocation of public funds to schools not under comprehensive public supervision as part of parental and communal autonomy.[29] The existence of such schools may meet the needs of cultural, ethnic, and religious or otherwise ideological diversity.

A district court, presiding as an administrative court said, in regarding one group of schools, from the ultra-orthodox sector, pinpointed this conflict in 2004. According to the court, the existence of private schools, side by side with the formal schools, is one of the characteristics of a participatory democracy. Such a government encourages communal organizations, and allows communities to organize their lives pursuant to their own understanding, and, among other things, by the operation of education institutions.

The court further noted that insofar as private schools answer the need for diversity and retaining uniqueness in a multicultural society, their doing so advances individual autonomy materialized by the ability to control education. An attempt to dictate educational content, the court thought, might severely harm such autonomy. The court further specified that mandating a uniform type of education might harm the unique needs of various communities while harming the wills to preserve their cultures and identities. The court explained that it could be stated that the complete prevention of private schools might harm human dignity, and in certain circumstances, the democratic fabric of life. Such prevention, the court concluded, might hurt the rights of minorities to organize as communities, when such rights are recognized.[30]

Still, if diversity is such a fundamental right, why grant it only to those affluent enough to afford private education? Therefore, after 2000, Israeli courts adopted a somewhat neoliberal viewpoint.

Israel's educational system succeeds in reaching high retention rates and one of the three highest from the top in accessibility to high-quality academic higher education worldwide.[31] Yet this educational success is not evenly dispersed among the various groups of Israel's society, especially not among Israeli-Palestinian, the Jewish ultra-orthodox populations, and in peripheral areas.

While Israel offers Jewish students and their parents the choice among three types of schools, according to degree and stream of religion, and supplies them in every place all over Israel, Palestinian-Israeli students have only one type of school.

This is an important aspect of fulfilling the right to education because government schools in Arabic provide comprehensive K–12 education on all subjects, including the final matriculation examinations granting accessibility to higher education. Such a complete school system for the entire population of an indigenous nation, in its language and culture, is not common in other democracies that sometimes offer only some form of partial, complementary such as a "Sunday School" model, of education in a different language, rather than the full range the system offers in its mainstream language. Yet this single government system in Arabic means that religious education is not covered by the government-maintained school system for Palestinian-Israelis.

Student Rights before 2000

In reviewing the state of students' rights in the pre-2000 era, Israel ratified the UNCRC in 1991,[32] thus amplifying the emerging debate on pupils' rights in schools, of which the linchpin was the Pupils' Rights Act (2000), the law at the core of this chapter and the base of empirical findings presented below. Before its enactment, students' rights were limited through the Ministry of Education's circulars and administrative directives. Further, a body of case law emerged in which general principles of Israel's constitutional law were applied, haphazardly, as appeals or petitions were forwarded especially to the Supreme Court, in its role as High Court of Justice, and sometimes in civil issues to district courts, and government disciplinary tribunals.

Typical issues of the right to education included six major sets of issues. The first issues concerned school choice and attempts to circumvent mandatory integration policy and attendance boundaries. The second set examined segregation in religious schools between Ashkenazi and Sephardi Jews. The third grouping focused on the approval of new schools outside of the state system. The next set reviewed assistance in receiving special education services.

The fifth addressed unreasonable, including corporal, punishment. Finally, the sixth set of issues examined some issues of free speech and political involvement of teachers.[33] Even so, students' rights to, in, and through education were not present in Israeli case law. This absence of legal debate over students' rights was largely due to the basic inequalities and areas of discrimination and marginalization of disenfranchised populations.

Israel ratified the UNCRC in 1991. Yet Israel's legal system is dualist, as opposed to monist, with regard to international public law. In other words, in monist systems, when state officials sign international documents into effect, they become part of national laws. In dualist systems, even after treaties are ratified, they are not automatically part of national laws. As such, the convention was not automatically become integrated in Israel's education law. However, the courts, and especially the Supreme Court, relied on the convention as an interpretive tool.

Meanwhile,[34] in 1997, the Ministry of Justice established a government committee[35] for the Implementation of the International Convention in Israeli Law comprised of multiple subcommittees, one of which devoted its report to education. The committee presented its report to the Minister of Justice in 2004. During the committee's debates, the Knesset accepted the Students' Rights Act (Act),[36] a move not coordinated by the committee. Nevertheless, the committee's report supported the Act while providing tailwind that enhanced public debate including within the education system.

The Students' Rights Act of 2000: An Overview

The Act is unique in the world, not perhaps in its content, but in its structure and formation. The Act is a single distinct piece of primary legislation that aspires to incorporate and establish as many aspects of students' rights as possible, both in Israel's legal system and in the schools and lives of students, school leaders, and school staff.

The idea of introducing and enacting students' rights act into Israel's school law and educational system did not occur in a political or pedagogical void. A variety of NGOs, including the Association for Civil Rights in Israel (ACRI), and the Israel National Council for the Child (NCC), an influential NGO advocating for legislation in the area of the rights of children, and a group of young activist attorneys[37] were part of the public awakening accompanying the Act.

Resistance and opposition to the Act came from two major interest groups. The first objecting group consisted of religious parties in the Knesset and religious schools, principals, and teachers. Theses opponents saw the Act as having a possible crippling effect on the perhaps authoritarian culture and nature of their schools, regarding specific structural and curricular issues such as religious worship, separation of boys and girls in schools, and different curricula for boys and girls, mainly deeper religious studies for boys. This sector was also worried that the Act might promote ideas and rights regarding alternative GLTBQ life styles. The ultra-orthodox sector was worried that because they teach less general academic subjects, critique toward possible obstruction of prospects of its graduates to pursue academic higher education, and better paying jobs might follow.

The teachers' unions were the second interest group opposed to the Act. Their resistance, not surprisingly perhaps, carried a narrative of anxiety from a legal-adversarial culture into schools and an apocalyptic vision of teachers and principals having to "lawyer up" against their students, unable to impose discipline, and losing respect.

The Act includes twenty-one articles divided into four distinct groups. The first group includes general declarative, sometimes "manifest" style introductory issues (articles 1 and 3). The second group includes previously recognized student rights that already existed in Israel's law when the Act was accepted, either through secondary legislation such as Article 5A, 6–8, 10, 11, directives and circulars, and/or though judicial orders and precedents or constitutional principles already established in Israel's legislation such as antidiscrimination laws of various kinds. The rights in this group were, therefore, either "upgraded" from the level of secondary legislation or judicial precedent to primary legislation.

The third group of rights can be labeled as "new" rights that were not previously recognized in Israel's constitutional, administrative, and educational law, in ministry directives and circulars and in court rulings (Articles 5A1–4, 9). These "new" rights are specific to life in schools, to teaching, learning, and pedagogy akin to the *lex specialis* which deals directly with grievances toward and shortcomings of life in schools. The courts, despite enormous contribution to the development of students' rights in Israel and elsewhere,[38] both in their opinions and as catalysts of new legislation, are still typically passive and incidental in their decision-making process, based and dependent, first, on people petitioning for judicial review rather than proactive policy. As such, this third group makes a major contribution to the rights discourse and the right to education in Israel's educational law.

The fourth group includes administrative and procedural directives and mandates on the implementation of the Act and its coverage and authority over various types of schools.

The Student's Rights Act 2000: Structure and Content

Three articles in the Act are most important: Article 3 establishes the right to education; Article 5 forbids discrimination; and Article 9 grants accessibility to government matriculation examinations. Following the previous differentiation of three types and origins of rights, each of the three represents one. Article 1 places the Act in context of the UNCRC by declaring its commitment to a balance between students and staff. Article 3 pinpoints the right to education. Article 5 includes both, that is rights "upgraded" from secondary legislation and case law, as well as "new" rights embedded in school life. Further, Article 9 represents the "new" type of rights as well.

THE TRADEOFF BETWEEN THE RIGHTS OF TEACHERS AND STUDENTS

The opposition of teachers to the Act needs to be considered in light of the context of their status and conflictual situation in Israel's education system. The government and municipal authorities employ the lion's share of the workforce. Two strong teacher unions represent these teachers. The ITU[40] represents some 200,000 members mainly in the primary and junior high sectors, as well as in academic teachers' colleges, and the SSTA[39] represents some 70,000 teachers in secondary schools.

Since the earliest days of the State of Israel, the members of these two unions, representing all but a fraction of the profession, enjoyed, and continue to enjoy, excellent terms of employment and high job security. This includes lifetime tenure, granted automatically, after three years of working over one-third of a full post with salaries updated mainly according to length of employment with minimal link to formal education or other forms of success/professional scrutiny and a full-pay, year-long sabbatical every six years.

After a national task force on education presented its report in 2005, there were some minute changes to the rights of teachers. Under these changes, principals received a bit more discretion to refuse to grant tenure to teachers in extreme cases. The task force also introduced a loose system of promotion for teachers. All of these conditions are protected via a statutory collective agreement between the unions and the government. Even so, teachers are still practically immune from any form of professionally based termination of employment.

The big change in the status of teachers, perhaps a result of having strong job security, was that gradually the state and various municipalities began hiring teachers on personal contracts. In big cities, special manpower supply companies were established to employ teachers with thousands of them employed through these. These teachers lacked the protections of tenure and often received poor salaries and per-hour contracts that can be renewed yearly without pay for holidays. The status of these teachers led to multiple labor disputes with the unions who had limited success to date in attempting to incorporate these outsourced teachers into the mainstream method of employment including the tenure track.

The outsourcing of education began with extracurricular subjects and gradually shifted, so that as of 2017, they can provide courses in mathematics, Hebrew, and English in primary schools, especially in poor areas, thus undermining the profession's status. Nevertheless, growing concern and critique toward the teachers' unions strengthen the attempts of the government to privatize and outsource teaching.

Amid these controversies, the media often present teachers as unaccountable and resistant to change, or any type of professional scrutiny. Parents are uneasy when principals explain that even in severe cases of educational malpractice, teachers cannot be fired and/or replaced. Within the teaching profession are voices claiming that outstanding teachers are not singled out and do not receive any type of bonuses, thereby resulting in an educational workforce prone to mediocrity.

Under the circumstances just described, Article 1 of the Act was amended on multiple occasions. The modifications led to the creation of a type of balance between the rights of students and teachers in an attempt to confront unions complaints that the Act disowns and abandons them, undermining their professional status and authority in schools. In Israel's public arena, there is ongoing debate linking teacher employment to the right to education or its lack thereof.

On the one hand, the strong job security teachers enjoy is seen as a factor designed to prevent improvements, rejuvenation, and reform in education. On the other hand, introducing market-based, semiprivatized teacher working conditions lowers the standards of education services, especially among dispossessed communities and minorities, creating a large unstable landscape with a high replacement rate in the workforce staffed by teachers who are constantly dissatisfied and feel discriminated.

Article 1 declares its commitment to student rights in light of the UNCRC, setting its role as an attempt to implement the Charter's goals. Article 1 was amended many times due to resistance from the teachers' unions. Initially, Article 1 had narrowed the scope of students' rights by "ensuring the uniqueness of different types of schools as defined in the Compulsory Learning Act and National Education Act," thus shielding religious education and religious schools from its provisions. In 2011, an amendment to Article 1 pledged to "protect the honor of the student, the education employee, and the staff of an educational institution."

In the language of this amendment to Article I, one can see the footprints of a popular, though challenging, equilibrium that places "rights" as opposed to and supplementing "duties." This popular philosophy is often evident when doctoral students and faculty members from higher educational institutions are invited to lecture on the Act in schools. Once the topic of the lecture is announced, usually by the principal, someone from the audience questions the need to talk about rights without talking about duties or asks about teacher's rights, complaining that it is all about student rights all of the time. Statements of this type reveal, in a nutshell, the lack of basic constitutional comprehension among many teachers. The Act has thus created both excitement and anxiety in schools, but to date no study has shown any change, negative or other, in discipline or student behavior, or of any weakening of the authority or status of teachers.

This balance is a misunderstanding of the idea of a right: institutions and persons of authority do not have "rights" vis-à-vis subordinates or recipients of services. Of course, employees have rights under labor law and are entitled to protection from and by their employers, but toward students, they are more like institutions, carriers of power. Therefore, the cry about teacher rights is irrelevant when discussing the rights of students. Teachers hold, ideally, the foremost responsibility for nurturing, promoting, developing, and safeguarding, the rights of students. At the same time, students are a vulnerable group of individuals, both as minors and as captive audiences within somewhat coercive institutions that are responsible for their well-being and personal growth.

THE RIGHT TO EDUCATION, THE ACT, AND DISCRIMINATION IN EDUCATION: A CONSTITUTIONAL TYPOLOGY

Article 3 of the Act, the second declarative article, anchors the "right to education for every child according to law." This is an important constitutional contribution as well as an addition to the Compulsory Learning Act of 1949 and the National Education Act of 1953. As explained, these statutes guaranteed government-maintained K–12 education, but never declared it to be a constitutional right or interest.[40] Article 3 changed that lack of interest in establishing the right to education, thereby "upgrading" court rulings specifying that this right exists, into primary legislation. The two declarative articles, 1 and 3 complement each other.

Article 4 requires educational officials to publicize the Act among the students in their schools at the opening of each academic year. However, educators follow this article only partially and sporadically. The good news is that the Act is well known among students and parents, due, among other factors, to social media, the work of ACRI and the NCC, and clinical departments in law schools witnessing the growing volume of requests for help from parents and students.

Article 5 addresses discrimination in schools. Nondiscrimination is a fundamental long-standing principle of Israel's constitutional and administrative law, the so-called material constitution after more than sixty-five years of Supreme Court rulings and some "Basic Laws."[41] Among the legislation utilized and adopted for safeguarding the rights of students are Basic Law: Human Dignity and Liberty[42] and the Forbidden Discrimination in Products, Services, Entry into Places of Entertainment and Public Places Act.[43] As useful and comprehensive as the protection under these laws is, along with the protection provided by case law safeguarding the rights of students, they can in no way compare to the significance and formality of Article 5 of the Students' Rights Act.

Article 5A introduces six cornerstones for discrimination: ethnic origin, country of origin, socioeconomic background, sexual orientation and gender identity, political viewpoint; all of these apply to either students and/or their parents. This list is not the original one from year 2000 when the Act was adopted. If anything, the list has gone through multiple changes. Sexual orientation and gender are recent additions, finally overcoming resistance from religious groups. Country of origin, contrary to national origin, was added to protect new immigrants, solely Jewish, but was phrased in a manner that will not provide protection against discrimination of Israeli-born Palestine citizens; the term *ethnic* in Israel is reserved for Sephardi versus Ashkenazi Jews only.

Palestinian-Israeli students are among the most, if not the most, vulnerable to discrimination in Israel's society. Accordingly, these students deserve special protection, especially within an empowering fundamental service like education, with implications for citizenship and democracy. Additionally, mentioning a specific area of discrimination within a law titled "Student Rights" has significant influence on changing school cultures, encouraging debate in schools, and alerting principals, teachers, counselors, parents, and students to be vigilant toward violations. Therefore, the absence of national origin as an item protecting students in antidiscrimination law remains regrettable.

Article 5A does not mention discrimination for religious reasons. This remains an issue in Israel's multireligious scene, with Jews, in various substantial streams, secular, orthodox, ultra-orthodox, reform, conservative, along with Muslims and Christians who might suffer from discrimination in education, with regard to curricular, cultural, and other types of diversity.

Finally, despite the welcome addition of forbidding discrimination for reason of sexual orientation and gender, this perhaps highlights the absence of the citing of illicit discrimination for reason of sex, again due to concerns by religious factions. Once more, pressure from Jewish religious groups prevented adding this reason for antidiscrimination to the Act.

It is imperative to stress that these lacunae or omissions in Article 5A do not mean that discrimination, for example, based on reasons of national origin, sex, or religion, are legal. Rather, the declarative factor and visibility in the Act dealing specifically with students' rights carries its weight such that adding these fields of discrimination to the law is an ongoing struggle by rights NGOs, legal and educational academics, and as a component part of public debate.

The instructional and educational, not just legal, factor in having a Students' Rights Act, and treating it as one of the few legal documents to be presented, read, and learned by the members of school staffs is a valid reason for concentrating the various antidiscrimination justifications within its provisions. Antidiscrimination principles and criteria are scattered in general constitutional and administrative law, in case law, and in secondary legal sources such as ministry directives and circulars which remain part of the training of legal scholars and perhaps of policymakers and superintendents. This scattershot approach renders these legal pronouncements much more difficult to embed in the daily discourse of schools. This approach also makes these legal pronouncements a true bill of rights for students.

Mapping the Educational Domain, Expulsion, Discipline, Privacy, Voice, and Jurisdiction

After mapping the causes for nondiscrimination in Article 5A, Article 5B lists four educational and pedagogical domains in which discriminatory practices are forbidden. The four domains are enrollment and exclusion in schools (5B1); curriculum programs and streaming (5B2); separate classrooms within the same educational institution (5B3); and student rights including discipline (5B4).

Article 5 is therefore a novelty from two aspects. First, by its incorporation of discrimination issues for Israel's constitutional, administrative, and case law into a specific law devoted to the rights of students in one package (5A). The second novelty is the list of the areas of forbidden discrimination; instead of leaving these issues open for judicial discretion, Article 5B lists new areas that are the result of measured scrutiny of discriminatory issues in actual school life. Article 5C also specifies that breaches of the discriminatory actions identified in its four domains are felonies punishable by incarceration.

Articles 6, 7, and 8 provide a framework of principles and processes of school exclusions. These articles belong to the "upgrade" group, namely those articles that adopted procedures already rooted in case law and/or in secondary legislation. The "upgrade" concentrates them in the Students' Rights Act. The articles are procedural in nature, but phrased in ways designed to ensures due process[44] in the face of expulsions, circumstances, and powers, appeals, and decisions.

Unfortunately, again, in 2011, due to growing pressures from teacher unions and a concern of imagined disciplinary problems in schools, these generally positive principles were amended. At the same time, an option for immediate permanent expulsion was introduced with the processes safeguarding the rights of students to education carried out ex post facto if pupils are permanently removed from schools. This addition is problematic with regard to the right to education because permanent expulsion from a school is the educational version of exile and can no longer be an accepted form of punishment in a democratic rights-based society.

Maintaining discipline in schools, a worthy and often essential practice, does sometimes require immediate educators to exclude students temporarily after officials provide students with due process; these exclusions can also turn into permanent removals. Temporary immediate exclusions can be necessary, for example, in cases of extreme violence and sexual harassment along with similar types of misconduct that cannot justify immediate permanent exclusion circumventing due process. This is especially true as to students who get mixed up in disciplinary issues are often of low-SES backgrounds or of marginalized ethnic groups that are much less aware of their procedural rights or whose parents sometimes do not understand Hebrew because they are immigrants and are wary of authorities, a phenomenon common to immigrants worldwide. The urgent quality of misconduct cannot be justified by the permanent aspect that is too severe when treating minors and their right to education.

Articles 10 and 11 place restrictions on punishment, forbidding corporal or humiliating punishment that contradicts human dignity, a term anchored in Israel's Basic Law: Human Dignity and Liberty, a common frame of reference. Further, Article 13 requires officials in educational institutions to encourage the establishment of students' councils.

Article Fourteen restricts the abuse of information gathered by holding posts as officials carrying out duties according to the its provisions, a right already present in Israel's law through the Privacy Protection Act, 1981.[45] Yet because this is addressed in specific sections of the Students' Rights Act, it may be subject to more attention in the everyday lives in schools. Article 16, which sets the scope of the Act's jurisdiction, limits some of its powers to the "Recognized-Formal"[46] schools only.

Other "education institutions," defined in the National Education Act as "Recognized Non-Formal," are exempt from abiding to articles 6, 7, and 13. This means that the large "Haredi" or ultra-orthodox sector and NGO-controlled schools comprising over a third of Israel's school system, yet receiving between 65 and 100 percent of public funds, are exempt from most of the due process requirements regarding suspensions and permanent exclusions as well as the obligation to set up student councils. This arrangement, again, is the result of negotiations and pressures from religious political parties that participated coalition governments, creates a two-tier system of rights in which basic rights recognized by law are reserved for some schools while other publicly maintained schools are exempt from these same requirements.

Comment and Critique of the Students' Rights Act: From the UNCRC to the Act

Legal scholars and civil rights organizations criticized the Act for not abiding fully with the International Convention. For instance, the Act does not include religious and sex-based discrimination aspects in Article 5, fails to address the issue of ethnic groups and not just birthplace, and overlooks issues of freedom of speech and demonstration as well as the rights of children to participate as individuals in decisions concerning them and their education. In fairness, though, it must be noted that, as originally proposed, the bill did address discrimination on the base of sex and national origin, it offered safeguards for students' freedom of speech and sought to involve students in decision concerning their well-being.

Parent groups and teacher unions criticize the Act from an opposite perspective. These critics view the Act as a serious threat to the authority of teachers that might expose children to violent peers by granting them immunity from disciplinary measures and encouraging disruptive behavior in classrooms, resulting in harming the right to education of others. Moreover, teacher unions cautioned that wealthy parents might use the Act to threaten teachers with litigation and consequently allow their children to do as they please.

The original bill also contained a detailed list of government obligations to provide services under compulsory schooling along with a proposed statutory council for the rights of pupils with powers to intervene in schools. However, these articles were removed from the final version of the bill. Pressures to remove these provisions from the bill came from four places. The treasury opposed these terms because it was against establishing an independently financed "watchdog" along with the detailed list of mandatory services in schools. Next, religious groups were opposed to these provisions based on their fear that specific mentions of religious discrimination might lead to petitions against them. Finally, the Ministry of Education, in worrying that its authority would have been be undermined, essentially backed the teachers' unions in opposing these provisions.

Still, the Act, even in its somewhat curtailed version, is a substantial contribution to Israel's scant body of school law, and was certainly sufficient to ignite ongoing, heated arguments. Teacher status being at a record low from many aspects became an issue vis-à-vis the Act. In light of this background, the law has subsequently been discussed in 111 cases during its first fifteen years of existence; these are analyzed in the next section of this chapter.

The Students' Rights Act and the Courts

One of the strong arguments against the Act was that the courts would seize the opportunity and use the new law, enacted in 2000, to impose problematic and contested norms on schools and educators. Educators, academics in education, and, of course, the teachers' unions and principals' organizations, painted a dark picture of the ramifications of the Act to discipline in schools, to the professional status of staff, and even to child safety due to supposed chaos that would reign once the Act was implemented.

The absurdity of judicial controversies was that the natural guardians of students' rights, teachers, were the most vehement opponents of the Act, rather than its initiators, catalysts, and/or protagonists. The disagreements created understandable curiosity as to what the courts would do once petitions based on the law began. However, my 2011 study summarizing the view of the courts for the first decade of the Act proved the opposite.[47] The results of this study revealed that the courts did not overturn the authority of teachers, did not provide immunity to children from affluent families, and did not disrupt life in schools.

Following my initial study, I set out to understand if and what has changed over the next five years, 2011 to 2015 inclusive. The results of the fifteen years of litigation over the Act, consistent with the initial findings, are summarized in table 2.1 and are discussed below.

The first finding in the study was that the eminent fear that courts would take over disciplinary actions in schools while limiting the limit the authority of educators and undermine professional status was seriously overrated. Judi-

Table 2.1. Court Rulings according to the Students' Rights Act: Concepts and Areas

Procedure /court	%	Subject/Issue	%	Articles Used	%
Civil rights petition to the high court of justice	19%	Recognition of nongovernment public school (charter, magnet, etc.)	17%	1—Applying the international UNCRC.	11.7%
Civil rights petition to a district court	44%	Permanent exclusion	10.8%	3—The right to education	45%
Civil procedure	20%	Transport, school allocation	16.2%	5—Forbidding discrimination	13.5%
Appeal to a municipal court	5.5%	Ethnic/SES-based discrimination; segregation/ desegregation	26%	6, 7—Suspension/ expulsion procedures	10%
Criminal procedure	4.5%	Retention, discipline, cruel/ unusual/humiliating punishment	14.4%	9—Accessibility to baccalaureate government exams	5.4%
Other	11.7%			10—Humiliating and unusual punishment	5.4%
				16—The law's incidence on nongovernment schools.	8.1%

N = 111

cial intervention in disciplinary issues including punishment and exclusions was minimal. In an overwhelming majority of cases, the courts rejected appeals and claims against the schools and educators, thereby supporting school policies and the educators. The courts strictly avoided interfering in pedagogical issues, reserving their limited interventions to matters of procedure and due process.

A word of caution though is appropriate here because it is unclear what the cultural or internal political influences the law had on schools, an issue that has never been studied empirically. This means that perhaps the sheer existence of the Act and the relatively few court cases might suffice to create anxiety among teachers and principals, causing them to consider and reconsider disciplinary actions, exclusions, or reactions to the behavior of students. This field thus calls for further research, not legal but sociological.

The second important finding is that rather than focusing on the practical and more technical or prescriptive articles of the Act, such as Article 5, the courts make frequent use of the general constitutional articles, 1 and 3. While article 5 is present in only 17.5 percent of the cases, Article 3, on the right to education, is mentioned as the basis for the judgments in 45 percent of decisions.

This can perhaps be explained by the relatively large proportion of cases presented to the Supreme Court in its capacity as High Court of Justice along with the growing number of constitutional appeals to district courts that comprise, together, some 60 percent of the cases.

Within this group of cases, the growing use of the district courts' relatively new constitutional powers, now decentralized from the Supreme Court to district level, is also interesting.[48] Because this procedure is faster and cheaper than petitioning the Supreme Court, it encourages petitions for "localized" judicial review. A byproduct of this constitutional and administrative change is growing interest in the right to education along with increased use of Article 1 and its commitment to the rights of students as well as the UNCRC and Article 3's focus on the right to education. This finding, one that is ongoing and consecutive from 2000 to 2016, is substantial and interesting.

The courts are proactive, in the sense that they view articles 1 and 3 not as introductory and decorative parts of the Act, but as major pathways to create a body of case law on the rights of students while serving as roadmap for policy makers and lower courts for fortifying and substantiating the right to education. Typical statements by the courts depict this trend:

> The interpretation of the Act (Article 3 "the right to education"—DG) is twofold and perhaps threefold. First, the right to education is anchored in the law and can be narrowed only according to law; second, the right to education is granted to every child on an equal base: one child's right cannot have prefer-

ence over another; third, implementing the right to education of one child can never be at the expense of realizing the right to education of another child.[49]

It's always problematic when equality is jeopardized, but it is sevenfold when the right to education is concerned.[50]

The right to education is not limited to the individual's right to choose education but includes a proactive duty on the authorities to allow this right to be fulfilled on an equal base.[51]

The right to education is a basic human right, part of a comprehensive concept of values on which Israel's society is based . . . the right of children to education has been fortified lately in the Pupils Rights Act.[52]

The right to education includes the right to receive education, choose education, influence contents of education and equality in education.[53]

DISCUSSION AND CONCLUSION

This chapter is largely limited to issues of the right to education in education law, along with its impact on teachers, rather than a wider debate on Israel's constitutional law and supreme/administrative court's powers of intervention in policy, separate and noteworthy issues. One can conclude that articles 1 and 3 of the Act have opened the door for important developments and contributions to Israel's students and more generally in the arena of the rights of children.

This consecutive development is a key promise to the right to education because it allows the further development of the right to education in the future, moving into uncharted territories, using the general authority the courts adopted through the declarative and manifest-style articles 1 and 3. This allows the courts to work with the legislature, as to new areas that must be addressed and to adopt new interpretations, new areas, and aspects of the right to education.

In one case, for instance, the Supreme Court ordered authorities to build a bridge over a path to a school that was swamped by a stream in a poor Bedouin "unauthorized" village receiving no government services because it was deemed "illegal." The court ruled that the rights of village children to receive their educations could not be compromised by the legal issues that arose over the status of the settlement.[54] In another recent landmark case, the Court intervened in an interview and examination enrollment process in one of the new specialized "Natural Sciences" schools that sprung up lately as part of the drive of affluent populations to distance themselves from the mainstream public schooling.[55]

The examples of Supreme Court cases are piling up. Even so, when taking an overall view of the implementation of Articles 1 and 3 of the Act over fifteen years, it is evident that the use of these two articles is weakening somewhat at the expense of its more specific provisions. This can be explained in a positive manner because perhaps when the Act was new, the courts thought they were compelled to "educate" the authorities by reinforcing and anchoring the right to education. Now, after a decade and a half, the courts are a bit more relaxed, although as can be seen from the last case, the judiciary remains vigilant and willing to explore new ground.

Following the establishment of Israel in 1948, the 1950s and 1960s witnessed legislation that founded the right to education without labeling it as such. The system allowed substantial choice and pluralism, perhaps creating severe inequalities. This is an issue in need of further attention, especially with regard to the Palestinian-Israeli population. Later on, the courts added to the right and expanded it, especially in their fierce defense of integration policies in the 1970s and 1980s. In year 2000, the Students Rights Act, in itself an impressive achievement in the field worldwide, allowed further development of the right to education along with the adaptation of the right to specific conditions in schools.

Implementation and preservation of the right to education in Israel is neither complete nor is it entirely equilibrated. Entering new areas, such as the rights of students to demonstrate and free speech, as well as allowing teachers further political involvement and freedom while recognizing new areas of protection from discrimination, especially due to national origin, sex and religion are required. Even so, the intensive debate and novelties in the field demonstrate that the Students' Rights Act has withstood serious attacks but emerged, and remains, as a sustainable part of Israel's constitutional law, thereby offering hope and measured optimism for the future.

NOTES

1. HCJ 1554/95 *Shocharei Gilat, NGO v. The Secretary of State for Education and Culture*, [1995] Isr HCJ 50 (3) 325.

2. Thompson-Ford, R., (2004). "Brown's Ghost." *Harvard Law Review* 117 (3), pp. 1305–33.

3. Harris, R., Kedar, A., Lahav,P., and Likhovsky, A. (eds.). *The History of Law in A Multi-Cultural Society: Israel 1917–1967*, p. 15 (Ashgate, 2002). See also Shachar, Y., "Jefferson Goes East: The American Origins of the Israeli Declaration of Independence." *Theoretical Inquiries in Law* 10.2 (2009).

4. Hodgkin, R., and Newell, P. (eds.) (2008). *Implementation Handbook for the Convention on the Rights of the Child* (3rd ed.), UNICEF.

5. Verhellen, E. (2001). "Facilitating Children's Rights in Education Expectations and Demands on Teachers and Parents." In Hart, S. N., Cohen, C. P., Erickson, M. F., and Flekkoy, M. (eds.) *Children's Rights in Education* (pp. 179–90). London: J. Kingsley Publishers; Verhellen, E. (2006). *Convention on the Rights of the Child: Background, Motivation, Strategies, Main Themes* (4th ed.), Garant Uitgevers nv; Jones, P., and Welch, S. (2010) *Rethinking Children's Rights: Attitudes in Contemporary Society*. New York: Continuum; Tan, J. (2011). "Education and Children's Rights." In Jones, P., and Walker, G. (eds.) (2011). *Children's Rights in Practice* (pp. 121–35). London: Sage.

6. Freeman, M. D. A. (1992). "Introduction: Rights' Ideology, and Children." Ch. 1 in Freeman, M. D. A. and Veerman, P. (1992) (eds.) *The Ideologies of Children's Rights* (3–28). Dordecht: Martinus Nijhoff; Raby, R. (2008). "Frustrated, Resigned, Outspoken: Students' Engagement with School Rules and Some Implications for Participatory Citizenship." *The*

International Journal of Children's Rights 16 (2008) 77–98; Thornberg, R. (2009) "Rules in Everyday School Life: Teacher Strategies Undermine Pupil Participation." *International Journal of Children's Rights* 17 (2009) 393–413.

7. Freeman, *supra* note 6, 3 (emphasis added).
8. *Supra*, note 5, Tan. J., 123.
9. Rawls, J. (1971). *A Theory of Justice*. Cambridge, MA: Belknap-Harvard University Press.
10. Nussbaum, M. C. (2006). *Frontiers of Justice: Disability, Nationality, Species Membership*. Cambridge, MA: Belknap-Harvard University Press, 76–78.
11. Brighouse, H. (2006). *On Education*. Milton Park, UK: Routledge.
12. Verhellen, *supra*, note 5.
13. Clark-Power, F., Power, A. M. R., Bredemeir, B. L., and Light-Shields, D. (2001). "Democratic Education and Children's Rights." Ch. 5 in Hart, S. N., Cohen, C. P., Erickson, M. F., and Flekkoy, M. (eds.) *Children's Rights in Education* (pp. 98–118). London: J. Kingsley Publishers. Gutmann, A. (1987), *Democratic Education*, Princeton, NJ: Princeton University Press. Heslep, R. D. (1989), *Education in Democracy: Education's Moral Role in the Democratic State*, Ames: State University of Iowa Press; Sehr, D. T. (1997), *Education for Public Democracy*, Albany: State University of New York Press. Whitson, J. A. (1991), *Constitution and the Curriculum*, London: Falmer Press.
14. Imber, M., Van-Geel, T., Blokhuis, J. C., Feldman, J. (2013). *Education Law* (5th ed.), New York: Lawrence Erlbaum.
15. *Supra*, note 5, Tan, J., 132.
16. Noddings, N. (1995). *Philosophy of Education*. Dimensions of philosophy series. Boulder, CO: Westview Press.
17. Dworkin, R. (2000). *Sovereign Virtue: The Theory and Practice of Equality*. Cambridge, MA: Harvard University Press.
18. Gewirtz, S. (1998). "Post-Welfarist Schooling: A Social Justice Audit." *Education and Social Justice* 1 (1) pp. 52–63.
19. Gillborn, D. (2008). *Racism and Education: Coincidence or Conspiracy*. Abingdon, UK: Routledge.
20. Abu-Asba, H. (2006) "Unsettled Issues in the Arab-Israeli Education System Before and After the Dovrat Report." In Inbar, D. (ed.) *Toward Educational Revolution?* Jerusalem: Van-Leer Institute, 248–61 (Hebrew).
21. National Education Act 1953, S.H. p. 137.
22. Compulsory Learning Act 1949, S.H. p. 287.
23. School Supervision Act, 1969, S.H. p. 564.
24. Special Education Act, 1988, S.H. p. 1256.
25. *Supra*, note 22.
26. Gibton, D. (2004). "A Comparative and Critical View on the High Court's Position on Integration in Israel's School System." *Tel-Aviv Law Review* 28.2, 473–516. (Hebrew).
27. See for instance: HCJ 152/71 *Mordechai Kremer et al., v. Jerusalem Municipality et al.*, [1971] IsrDC 767; HCJ 595/88 *Chava Shulman v. School superintendent of Tel-Aviv Municipality et al.*, [1988] IsrDC 594; HCJ 986/05 *Shmuel Peled v. Tel-Aviv Municipality*. [2005].
28. Ichilov, A. (2010) "The Establishment of Public Education in Israel and the Withdraw from It." In Ichilov, A. (ed.) *Privatization and Marketization in public Education in Israel*. Tel-Aviv, Israel: Ramot/Tel-Aviv University, 21–51 (Hebrew).
29. HCJ 4363/00 *The local committee of Poria-Elite et al. v. the Minister of Education et al.* [2000] IsrDC (3) 3114. AA 35243-03-10 *The Association of the Followers of Husni Al-Kasami and the Parents Organization in Al-Kasami School v. The ministry of education* [2011].
30. AA 001320/03 *Menahem-Mendel Elkaslasi et al., v. Beitar-Ilit Municipality and the Ministry of Education, Section 10* [2004].
31. OECD (2014), Education at a Glance 2014: OECD Indicators, OECD Publishing. http://dx.doi.org/10.1787/eag-2014-.
32. Levush, R. (2007). 2007-04112 Law Library of Congress Israel Children's Rights: International and National Laws and Practice. Morag, T. (2006). "Court Rulings after Israel's

Ratification of the UNCRC: A New Era Indeed?" *HaMishpat Law Review of the The College of Management's Haim Stricks School of Law*, vol. 22, p. 21–32 (Hebrew).

33. Gibton, D. (2010). "The Role of Legislation in Advancing Social Justice in Educational Reform: Comparing England, the US, and Israel." In Hacker, D., Ziv N. *Does Law Matter?* Tel-Aviv: The Buchmann Faculty of Law, Tel-Aviv University (Hebrew).

34. Morag, T. (2010). "The Influence of the Committee for the Implementation of the UNCRC in Israel's Law in Israel's Court Rulings." *The Family Law* 2010, pp. 67–96.

35. *Ministry of Justice Committee on the Implementation of the International Treaty on Children's Rights*. (Head: Hon. Savyona Rotlevi, Head of Subcommittee on Education: Prof. Orit Ichilov).

36. S.H. p. 42. The Act was the result of an imitative lead by former MK, minister, and deputy PM, Silvan Shalom.

37. Mrs. Yael Kafri, Adv.; Mrs. Yael Ayalon, Adv.

38. See in the US: Cambron-McCabe, N. H., McCarthy, M. M., and Thomas, S. B. (2009) *Public School Law: Teacher's and Student's Rights*, (6th ed.) Boston: Allyn & Bacon. In the UK: Harris, N. (2007) *Education, Law, and Diversity*. Oxford, UK: Hart Publishing.

39. ITU: Israel's Teachers Union; SSTA: Secondary Schools Teacher Association.

40. On the distinction between the two please see: Thompson-Ford, R. (2004). "Brown's Ghost." *Harvard Law Review* 117 (3), pp. 1305-33.

41. Rubinstein, A., and Medina, B. (2005). *Israel's Constitutional Law*. (6th ed.), Tel-Aviv, Israel: Schocken Books (Hebrew).

42. S.H. [1992] p. 1391.

43. S.H. [2000] p. 1765.

44. *Supra*, note 40, Cambron-McCabe et al., p. 229–32.

45. S.H. [1981] p. 1011.

46. National Education Act, *supra*, note 22, Article 1.

47. Gibton, D. (2012). "To Which Students Does the Law Care? Israel's Students' Rights Law, Its Contribution and Role and in the Eyes of the Courts." *Law & Business Review* 14, pp. 767–801.

48. Administrative and constitutional powers of district courts are an ongoing process, not reserved for cases of education law, but education is one of the areas affected, in a positive way, by these additional powers of district courts.

49. Tel-Aviv DC 2426/09 *Konfiden v. Roe (minor)* [2009] Judge Mudrik.

50. HCJ 2599/00 *"Yated" the organization for children with Down Syndrome v. The Ministry of Education* [2000], Justice Dorner.

51. HCJ 7374/01 *Roe v. The Ministry of Education*, [2001], Justice Prokachya.

52. HCJ 4363/00 *Poriya-Elite parents association v. The Minister of Education and Beit Yerah high school*, [2000] Justice Prokachya.

53. Tel-Aviv DC35243-03-10 *Al-Kasami and the parents association of Al-Kasami Secondary school v. The Ministry of Education* [2010] Judge Agmon-Gonen.

54. HCJ 3511/02 *The Association for Co-Habitation in the Negev, the Forty Association, the Communal Council of Um-Batin v. The Ministry of National Infrastructure et al.* [2003].

55. AA 6560-10-15 *Roe v. the State of Israel, the Ministry of Education and Sports, Tel-Aviv Municipality, the School of Nature and Environmental Studies in Tel-Aviv* [2015].

CASES

Tel-Aviv DC35243-03-10 *Al-Kasami and the parents association of Al-Kasami Secondary school v. The Ministry of Education* [2010].

HCJ 3511/02 *The Association for Co-Habitation in the Negev, the Forty Association, the Communal Council of Um-Batin v. The Ministry of National Infrastructure et al.* [2003]

AA 35243-03-10 *The Association of the Followers of Husni Al-Kasami and the Parents Organization in Al-Kasami School v. The ministry of education*. [2011].

HCJ 595/88 *Chava Shulman v. School superintendent of Tel-Aviv Municipality et al.* [1988] IsrDC 594.

HCJ 4363/00 *The local committee of Poria-Elite et al. v. the Minister of Education et al.* [2000] IsrDC (3) 3114.

AA 001320/03 *Menahem-Mendel Elkaslasi et al. v. Beitar-Ilit Municipality and the Ministry of Education, Section 10* [2004].

HCJ 152/71 *Mordechai Kremer et al. v. Jerusalem Municipality et al.*, [1971] IsrDC 767.

HCJ 4363/00 *Poriya-Elite parents association v. The Minister of Education and Beit Yerah high school* [2000].

HCJ 7374/01 *Roe v. The Ministry of Education* [2001].

AA 6560-10-15 *Roe v. the State of Israel, the Ministry of Education and Sports, Tel-Aviv Municipality, the School of Nature and Environmental Studies in Tel-Aviv* [2015].

HCJ 986/05 *Shmuel Peled v. Tel-Aviv Municipality* [2005].

HCJ 1554/95 *Shocharei Gilat, NGO v. The Secretary of State for Education and Culture* [1995] Isr HCJ 50 (3) 325.

HCJ 2599/00 *"Yated" the organization for children with Down syndrome v. The Ministry of Education* [2000].

Chapter Three

Palestine

Akram Daoud[1] and Lucy Royal-Dawson

INTRODUCTION

A description of the law regulating education in Palestine must start with a delineation of the territory under consideration. Some consider Palestine to refer to the area of land that lies between the Mediterranean Sea and the Jordan River while others do not recognize it as a separate, autonomous territory at all. The legal status of Palestine as a state remains contentious: it has nonmember observer state status at the United Nations as the State of Palestine (UN General Assembly, 2012). Yet while the Palestinian territories remain under Israeli military occupation, its state authorities cannot exercise all of the powers associated with full sovereignty.

For the purposes of this chapter, the area under discussion is the West Bank and the Gaza Strip. These are the territories over which the Palestinian National Authority (PNA) was conferred jurisdiction under the terms of the Declaration of Principles on Self-Government Arrangements in 1993, known as Oslo I. However, East Jerusalem, home to 400,000 Palestinians, was excluded from the jurisdiction of the PNA because it was one of the "issues that will be negotiated in the permanent status negotiations," along with other matters of contention (Oslo I, 1993, Article IV). While the PNA has no administrative institutions in East Jerusalem, its Ministry of Education and Higher Education supervises education there while its schools adhere to Palestinian education law. This chapter thus includes East Jerusalem.

The legal gray area of the application of Palestinian education law to East Jerusalem is just one of the many complications related to the PNA's legal and administrative responsibilities for education. The PNA retains legal and administrative responsibility for Palestinian learners who live beyond its jurisdiction in the areas of the West Bank containing Israeli settlements, and for the Palestinian prisoners in detention in Israeli prisons. Also, for Palestinians who have been physically separated by the Separation Wall from schools in the West Bank. Contributing to the complexity of the continued military occupation is the political division between the Palestinian authorities governing in the West Bank and Gaza Strip where separate legal frameworks are being developed.

It may seem odd to start an introduction to education law with a territorial description, but in the context of Palestine, the physical and administrative territorial divisions have resulted in a fantastically complicated situation which has a direct impact on the definition of legal jurisdiction and on legal enforcement. To start this introduction with the legal provision may risk giving the impression of a direct correspondence between legislation and jurisdiction, which would be misleading.

This chapter first discusses the patchwork of legal jurisdictions and the gray areas that resulted from prolonged military occupation and political divisions. It then introduces the law which regulates education and its imperfect reach to the patchwork of jurisdictions. Next, the chapter turns to the substantive characteristics of education under the Palestinian jurisdiction, visiting student and staff rights. It is a cautionary tale rather than an exemplar.

TERRITORY, JURISDICTION, AND LEGAL PROVISION FOR EDUCATION

As to education, the PNA holds legal and administrative responsibility for Palestinian learners who live within its legal jurisdiction. It also retains responsibility for some Palestinian learners who live beyond its legal jurisdiction. These areas span only some parts of the West Bank, and all of the Gaza Strip. The areas in which Palestinians live currently number eleven distinct territorial compartments, not including those who live in Syria, Lebanon, Jordan, and farther afield. The eleven compartments are: the Gaza Strip; Area A of the West Bank; Area B of the West Bank; Area C of the West Bank; East Jerusalem; enclaves inside East Jerusalem under PNA administration; enclaves outside East Jerusalem under the administration of the Jerusalem Municipality; H2—the area of Hebron City under Israeli control; the Seam Zone; refugee camps in the West Bank and the Gaza Strip; and Israeli prisons.

In order to allow a discussion of the legal protection for education, a brief description of each type of compartment follows. This is intended to provide context to the discussion of relevant legislation and legal jurisdiction which comes after.

The Gaza Strip

The Gaza Strip is the narrow piece of land measuring seven miles along Egypt's border by thirty-two miles between Israel's border and the Mediterranean Sea. It was estimated by the Palestinian Central Bureau of Statistics (PCBS) to be home to 1.85 million Palestinians (PCBS, 2015). Prior to its occupation by Israel in 1967, the area had been occupied by Egypt since 1948 with Egyptian law being applied. In 2005, Israel withdrew its settlers and military from the Gaza Strip, but retained control over the crossings between Gaza Strip and Israel, Gazan airspace, territorial waters, and the population register (B'Tselem, 2014). Israel's military law ceased to apply and the Gaza Strip became subject to Palestinian law (Cavanaugh, 2007).

If a Palestinian from the Gaza Strip is arrested and detained by Israel, he or she is processed under Israeli domestic law, not military law. Israel's residual control is deemed sufficient for the Gaza Strip to retain the status of occupied territory (UN General Assembly, 2013; Dinstein, 2009).

In 2007, the political faction Hamas took over the governing authority and broke away from the Ramallah-based Fatah-led government. Since then, the Gaza Strip has been under a blockade imposed by Israel. Entry of people and goods into and out of the Gaza Strip is tightly controlled, which hampers day-to-day life, humanitarian activities, and reconstruction after the hostilities in 2014.

Areas A, B, and C of the West Bank

The West Bank is the kidney-shaped area with its eastern border on the western bank of the Jordan River and western flank bordering Israel. Its border mostly, but not entirely, follows the Green Line which was the line drawn between Israel and Jordan after the war in 1948 to demarcate territorial claims. The total population of the West Bank was estimated in 2015 to be 2.9 million (PCBS, 2015). This figure is for the population of the West Bank and it includes East Jerusalem, its enclaves, the Seam Zone, refugees, and the prison population.

The Declaration of Principles on Interim Self-Government Arrangements, known as Oslo I, of 1993 and the subsequent Israeli-Palestinian Interim Agreement on the West Bank and the Gaza Strip, known as Oslo II, of 1995 were signed by Israel and the Palestinian Liberation Organization as the representative of the Palestinian people. The agreements transferred authority over many aspects of civil life from Israel to the newly established Palestinian National Authority (PNA), including education.

Under the Oslo II agreement (Oslo II, Chapter 2, Article XI), the territory of the West Bank and East Jerusalem was divided into three areas: Area A which incorporates Palestinian towns and land and is under full Palestinian civil and security control; Area B which includes Palestinian towns and land and is under Palestinian civil control and joint Israeli-Palestinian security control; and Area C which covers East Jerusalem, Israeli settlements in the West Bank, the roads between them and the Israeli military areas in the Jordan Valley. It is under full Israeli civil and security control.

The territorial divisions were made on the basis of demographics (B'Tselem, 2013). Areas A and B include Palestinian population centers and comprises 40 percent of the territory, fragmented into 166 pockets of habitation lying within the West Bank with some enclaves disconnected from each other. Area C is contiguous, both with itself and with Israel. It contains 125 settlements, home to approximately 350,000 settlers not including the settlements of East Jerusalem and Hebron (B'Tselem, 2015a).

Under the terms of the Oslo II agreement, Palestinians are not permitted to enter Area C while Israeli civilians are not allowed to enter Areas A and B. Despite this, Area C incorporates villages and homes to over 300,000 Palestinians, approximately 10 percent of the Palestinian population in the West Bank (United Nations Office for the Coordination of Humanitarian Affairs for the occupied Palestinian territories—UN-OCHA, 2014). These people who live in Area C have to travel to Areas A or B to access services, such as education, which often necessitates passing through a checkpoint controlled by the Israeli military.

East Jerusalem and Its Enclaves

East Jerusalem is part of the Palestinian territory of the West Bank that Israel has occupied since 1967 (International Court of Justice, 2004, para. 78). Its territorial demarcation was first made at the end of the 1948 war when it was occupied by Jordan and the Green Line separated it from Israeli-held West Jerusalem. Since 1967, the territorial demarcation of East Jerusalem has become highly contentious. Israel extended its law over the whole of Jerusalem, incorporating East Jerusalem which is considered by the international community as de facto annexation (UN General Assembly, 2013). The Jerusalem municipal borders now extend well beyond the Green Line into the West Bank.

The Palestinian population of East Jerusalem is just over 400,000, accounting for 60 percent of the population. The remaining 40 percent of the population are settlers (B'Tselem, 2015b). The majority of Palestinian residents do not have full Israeli citizenship, but have permanent residency rights, and hold a Jerusalem identity card (UN-OCHA, 2011a). Since 2004, East Jerusalem has been physically separated from the rest of the West Bank by the Separation Wall. In general, residents of East Jerusalem who hold the Jerusalem identity card can pass through the checkpoints in the Wall to travel to Ramallah or other parts of the West Bank, but West Bank identity card holders can only pass through the Wall into East Jerusalem if they have a permit issued by the Israel civil authority.

To complicate matters, the route of the Wall trapped some West Bank identity card holders in enclaves on the East Jerusalem side of the Wall; these people, approximately 1,600, require special permits to live in their homes and special coordination procedures to access services in East Jerusalem. In addition, approximately 55,000 East Jerusalem identity card holders were trapped in enclaves on the West Bank side of the Wall, separating them from services in East Jerusalem and creating a vacuum in service provision in that they are beyond the Wall and deemed beyond the Jerusalem Municipality's reach (UN-OCHA, 2011a).

H2—The Area of Hebron City under Israeli Control

Under the terms of the Oslo II agreement, the municipal area of Hebron was divided into two areas (Oslo II, 1995, Annex 1 Protocol Concerning Redeployment and Security Arrangements). H1, approximately 80 percent of the municipal area, was placed under the full administrative and security control of the PNA, akin to Area A of the rest of the West Bank. H2 contains the Old City, religious sites important to both Jews and Muslims, and four Israeli settlements. It was placed under the security control of Israel and civil responsibilities were placed under the authority of the PNA, except for the Israeli settler population, who are administered by the Israel Military Authority. The area is home to approximately 40,000 Palestinians and 500 Israeli settlers. The area is encircled by Israeli military checkpoints controlling the movement of the Palestinian population, who additionally are habitually the targets of violence from the settler population (UN-OCHA, 2013).

The Seam Zone

When, in 2004, Israel started to build the Separation Wall between the West Bank and Israel, its route detoured away from the Green Line and encroached on the West Bank to incorporate Israeli settlements. In doing so, it traps about 6,500 Palestinians between the Green Line and the Wall in what is known as the Seam Zone (UN-OCHA, 2011b). These people effectively live in Israel but do not have permission to do so unless they apply for a permit to be allowed to live in their own homes. They have to pass through the Wall to access services, such as education and healthcare, in Areas A and B of the West Bank.

Refugee Camps

In East Jerusalem, the West Bank and Gaza Strip, two million registered refugees live in twenty-seven refugee camps administered by the UN Relief and Works Agency for Palestinian Refugees in the Near East, known as UNRWA. The residents are the people who fled their homes in 1948 and 1967 and their descendents (UNRWA, 2014). The Gaza Strip is home to 1.25 million refugees, making up two-thirds of the Gaza Strip population. The West Bank and East Jerusalem have 787,000 refugees, just under a third of the population (PCBS, 2015).

Israeli Prisons

The inclusion of Israeli prisons and detention centers as a geographical compartment may seem an anomaly, but the sheer numbers of Palestinians who are arrested and detained by Israel's military warrants closer attention to their situation. In February 2016, there were 7,000 detainees (Addameer, 2016). An estimated 800,000 people have been detained since 1967, approximately one in five of the population (Addameer, 2014) and an estimated 500 to 700 children are arrested every year, most of whom are school students (Defense for Children International—Palestine Section [DCI/PS], 2015).

The previous section described the different physical and territorial situations in which Palestinians live. They connote the different realities facing Palestinians depending on where they live or find themselves. This discussion is relevant when considering the legal protections for education for Palestinians because different laws apply according to the fragmented spaces in which schools are located. The next section introduces the legal protections and their applicability in the fragments.

SOURCES OF EDUCATION LAW AND ITS APPLICATION

Palestinian Education Law

Under the Oslo Accords, control was transferred from the Israeli military government and its civil administration to Palestinian authorities over social and civil functions such as education and culture, health, social welfare, direct taxation, and tourism. Higher education was different because it evolved outside the control of the Israeli civil authorities before the Oslo process and thus did not need to be transferred.

The Ministry of Education and Higher Education (MOEHE) was among the first ministries to be established in August 1994 (Nicolai, 2007). Initially, laws dating back to the Jordanian occupation of the West Bank and the Egyptian occupation of the Gaza Strip from 1948 to 1967 were applied when the Ministry was first established. It was thought at the time that the final status negotiations for the occupied territories including East Jerusalem would have a bearing on the law's eventual content and scope and, as a consequence, it would be better to wait.

Absent progress toward a final status settlement, a national education law has now been drafted. However, it is under its third review and has not yet been endorsed by the executive body, the Palestinian Legislative Council. The Council was dissolved in 2007 after the arrest and detention by Israel of many parliamentarians, thus freezing lawmaking (PNA, 2010). In the meantime, the preexisting Jordanian Education Law no. 16 of 1964 applies in the West Bank Areas A and B. In Gaza, the Ministry of Education enacted a new law.

To complicate matters, the political separation between the West Bank and the Gaza Strip precipitated a unilateral move by the de facto governing authority in the Gaza Strip to promulgate its own education regulation in March 2013, the Education Law of 2013. It was met with criticism for driving a wedge in the legal governance for education between the two territories as each of the two territories has its own law for education (Palestinian Centre for Human Rights, 2013).

It is encouraging to read in the MOEHE's Education Development Strategic Plan 2014–2019 (2014) that one of its aims is to finalize and have approved by the cabinet a national education law by the end of 2016. Still, the plan does not explicitly discuss moves to reconcile disparities in the legal frameworks for education between the Gaza Strip and the West Bank.

Despite the political rift, some operational cooperation at the ministry level has been possible, with the Gaza Strip authorities being invited to comment on the West Bank authorities' latest development plan. Even so, the disparities in the legal frameworks remain.

A variety of other laws have a bearing on education. Palestine's Amended Basic Law of 2003, Article 24, provides every citizen the right to compulsory, free education until the end of the basic level (aged fifteen to sixteen). The law tasks the PNA with the supervision of all levels and institutions of education, including private educational institutions which are required to comply with the curriculum approved by the PNA. Further, it guarantees the independence of universities, institutes of higher education, and scientific research centers. It applies in both the West Bank and the Gaza Strip (UN Human Rights Council, 2008). Further, the Law for the Rights of the Disabled No. 4 of 1999 protects the right of all people with disabilities to education.

Higher education is regulated by the Higher Education Law No. 11 of 1998. It provides for the possibility of every citizen to access higher education and regulates the management and structure of higher education institutions.

Palestinian Child Law No. 7 of 2004 is closely aligned to the Convention of the Rights of the Child. Provision for the right to education is given in five articles. Article 37 extends free education to the end of secondary school, two years longer than the provision in the Amended Basic Law (2003) but maintains education to be compulsory until the end of the basic level. Article 38 requires that discrimination in accessing the right to education be eliminated with the aim of achieving equal opportunities for all children.

The participation of children and their parents in all decisions affecting them is protected in Article 39, along with efforts to ensure the dignity of the child in all programs affecting him or her. The child's rights to rest, leisure, and play, as well as cultural and artistic endeavors, are protected in Article 40. Article 41 outlines protections for children with disabilities and affords them the right to inclusive education, and those with exceptional disabilities are entitled to special classes or centers.

Other sources of legal protection pertaining to education are the Labour Law No. 7 of 2000, which applies to employees of private and nongovernmental institutions, the Civil Service Law of 1998, which applies to employees of government-run institutions, and the Publications and Copyright Law of 1911, which applies to all.

The laws not specific to education discussed here apply to Areas A and B of the West Bank, the Gaza Strip, and the refugee camps of both areas, but not to Israeli prisons where Palestinian prisoners are within Israeli jurisdiction. Further, there is a gray area with regard to the jurisdiction, implementation, and enforcement of Palestinian law in East Jerusalem and its enclaves, Area C, the Seam Zone, and H2 of Hebron. These gray areas are now discussed in more detail.

Education Law in East Jerusalem

Under the Oslo process, East Jerusalem and its status was put on the list of issues to be dealt with as part of the final status negotiations along with the settlements, return of refugees, security arrangements, and border control (Oslo I, 1993, Article V). Thus, PNA does not have legal jurisdiction over East Jerusalem even though in the eyes of the Palestinians and the international community it is part of occupied Palestine.

When Israel extended its legal jurisdiction to the whole of East Jerusalem in 1967, it was understood to be taking responsibility for providing education services to Palestinian children, too. Israel's Compulsory Education Law of 1949 entitles every child between the ages of five and sixteen living in Israel to free compulsory education. This provision applies to Palestinian children living in Jerusalem with the status of permanent resident.

The Jerusalem Municipal Education Authority (MANHI), the body responsible for the city's education, has been found in breach of its obligations in several rulings delivered by the Israeli High Court of Justice. The Court ordered MANHI to build sufficient infrastructure to accommodate all children entitled to a public education within five years.[2] According to Ir Amim and Association for Civil Rights in Israel [ACRI] (2012), two Israeli human rights organizations, MANHI continues to renege on its obligations despite this court ruling.

Even though the PNA's legal authority does not extend to East Jerusalem, MOEHE supervises over 100 schools in East Jerusalem. However, the PNA cannot provide direct services in Jerusalem and its ability to operate in Jerusalem is limited (PNA, 2010). PNA-schools are run by the Islamic Waqf, the foundation which stewards the Islamic holy places in Jerusalem. Other schools which are supervised by MOEHE are run by private foundations or UNRWA. Some Palestinian children attend schools run or supervised by the Israeli Jerusalem Municipal Education Authority.

One of the consequences of this mosaic of education provision is the absence of a unified school supervision system in East Jerusalem (Civic Coalition for Defending the Palestinians' Rights in Jerusalem, 2008). There is no system to monitor classroom teaching, curriculum implementation, progression, or dropout rates using the same criteria or method, and data collection is uncoordinated between the different providers. Moreover, compliance with legal obligations is not fully monitored.

The PNA wants to maintain a firm hold on education provision in East Jerusalem. Yet increasing numbers of Palestinian students are reportedly taking up places in MANHI schools which offer the Israeli curriculum (Hasson, 2012). Following the Israeli curriculum increases students' chances of accessing Israeli universities which would lead to qualifications recognized in Israel. Qualifications issued by the main Palestinian higher education institution operating in East Jerusalem, Al Quds University, are not recognized in Israel. Thus, an Israeli-accredited degree increases work opportunities.

The situation of education in East Jerusalem is complicated and paradoxical. The PNA has no legal jurisdiction but seeks to promote its control over education there. MANHI has legal responsibility but has been found in breach of its obligations. Accommodating all Palestinian learners would place a huge strain on resources and political motivation to act is weak. Pressure is high on children to attend schools offering Israeli curricula but Palestinian learners who attend them risk being labeled as unsympathetic toward the Palestinian cause. Pressure on MANHI to provide additional services for Palestinian children is at once resisted by the PNA and unattractive to MANHI. Yet the patchwork approach to the provision of education to Jerusalem's Palestinian children is a breach to their right to education.

The nebulous legal status of East Jerusalem does little to strengthen legal protection for the people living there. Indeed, it serves to erode trust in the law. The administration of education is not helped by the ill-defined legal jurisdiction.

Education in Area C and the Seam Zone

Many of the complexities related to legal protections for education evident in East Jerusalem are also present in Area C and the Seam Zone of the West Bank. The PNA has no legal jurisdiction but cannot ignore its responsibility for the education of Palestinian inhabitants of Area C and the Seam Zone. MOEHE operates more than 100 schools in these areas.

Palestinian children and other learners who live in these areas have reported difficulty accessing their schools. Harassment, delays, circuitous journeys to get round Israeli settlements, attacks by settlers and children being taken out of school for their own safety are commonly reported (United Nations General Assembly and Security Council, 2015). The route of the Wall has cut many families off from hospitals, schools, their families and land, and the restricted access has taken away major sources of income.

Learners who live on the Israeli side of the Wall, but study in the West Bank territory have to cross through the Wall and are exposed to harassment as well as delays. Violence and sexual abuse toward women and girls en route to school or university, both at checkpoints and in public transport, is often a reason for families give to prevent their daughters from studying further (Shalhoub-Kevorkian, 2008). Israeli authorities served demolition orders on eighteen schools in Area C because they were built without permits which are very difficult to obtain (UN-OCHA, 2011b). Khirbet Tana school was demolished twice in 2010.

So-called fragile indicators have been included in the monitoring and evaluation framework for the Education Development Strategy Plan for primary and secondary education in Area C to keep abreast of the attacks and lost education (MOEHE, 2014). The indicators include the number of schools exposed to military aggression, attacks on staff and students, hours of schooling lost due occupation-related incidents, and dropout rates. There is little MOEHE can do to prevent these incidents. Accordingly, its strategy is to monitor them and engage support from international partners.

Education in Hebron City Center

Within the separated area of the city of Hebron known as H2, about thirty schools operate under the supervision of MOEHE. As with life in H2 generally, access for children within H2 to some of these schools is characterized by harassment and violence, both from the Israeli Defense Force and settlers. The IDF are charged with keeping settlers and Palestinians apart, but often they are reported as doing nothing or supporting settlers when Palestinians come under attack (B'Tselem, 2015c). The MOEHE is in no position to protect the children. It monitors the violence and reports it under the fragile indicators, as in Area C and the Seam Zone.

UNRWA and Education in the Refugee Camps

The PNA's legal and judicial jurisdiction extends to the refugee camps even though it does not have full control of education services provided in these camps. Registered refugees are to abide by and respect all laws of the host country; the services provided to refugees, such as education, are delivered by UNRWA. Of the 2,753 schools operating in the occupied Palestinian territories, 344 are run by UNRWA, providing services to 24 percent of the school population (MOEHE, 2013). UNRWA is an agency of the United Nations, not of the Palestinian authorities, and it reports directly to the UN's General Assembly.

There is coordination between the MOEHE and UNRWA. For example, the government curriculum is taught in UNRWA schools and they comply with school monitoring requirements, but MOEHE cannot direct UNRWA's activities. Any legal violations by UNRWA are dealt with at the diplomatic level, rather than domestically. The services provided by UNRWA ease the demand for educational services on MOEHE, and are welcomed by the PNA but come at the cost of awkward administration requirements and diminished control. MOEHE would like to see improvement in coordination, particularly with regards to planning (MOEHE, 2014).

Legal Responsibility for the Education of Detainees and Ex-detainees

As mentioned above, hundreds of thousands of Palestinians have been arrested and convicted of a security-related or criminal offense under Israeli military or domestic law. Many of these people have been subject of breaches of multiple rights, documented elsewhere, such as the UN Human Rights Council (2013), including the denial of education in detention.

The Tel Aviv District Court in 1997 ruled that Palestinian children in Israeli detention have the same right to education as Israeli children in detention and that the Palestinian curriculum should be permitted.[3] However, the court decide that because the right was "subject to the security situation," it thus could be withheld if the situation so required. Provision of education to child prisoners is patchy, with only one prison reportedly providing education out of eleven interrogation or detention centers where children are held (DCI/PS, 2012). Those receiving education, namely those younger than sixteen, receive a limited curriculum not in conformity with the Palestinian curriculum and for only four hours a day. Like adult prisoners, child prisoners awaiting trial or in administrative detention receive no education.

The age of adulthood for Palestinian children is set at sixteen and above according to Military Order 1651[4] and at eighteen for non-Palestinian prisoners. Consequently, Palestinian children aged between sixteen and eighteen receive no education in Israeli prisons (Addameer, 2010). Many child prisoners are aged sixteen to eighteen and many of them are school students at the time of their arrest. These children have no opportunity to sit the general secondary school examinations (*tawjihi*).

Israel's responsibility for rehabilitative services does not extend to Palestinian ex-detainees because the Palestinian Ministry of Detainees and Ex-Detainees' Affairs (MODEDA) attends to their reintegration and rehabilitation. Ex-detainees often do not re-enroll into formal education. In this regard, Addameer (2010) reports that ex-detainees are poorly served by the efforts of MOEHE and MODEDA to help them back into education.

The psychological difficulties which ex-detainees develop require considerable resources that MODEDA lacks. Similarly, the interruption in their education requires specialist attention from an already financially constrained MOEHE. The periods of incarceration impact not just on education lost while inside, but also on subsequent attempts to continue with it. The Palestinian authorities have to respond to the needs of the ex-detainees, but have few resources to adequately provide for them.

Section Summary

This section has discussed the legal protection for education and the gray areas in its application to the Palestinian population. The fragmented territory and the dislocated population diminish the efficacy and even possibility of legal authority and enforcement. A unified or uniform application of education law to the Palestinian population is not possible with the fragmented nature of the territory and the divisions created under the regime of military occupation and the terms of the Oslo Accords.

A significant proportion of the Palestinian population, those living in East Jerusalem, Area C, the Seam Zone, parts of Hebron City, and Israeli prison are under less than full legal protection for education. Thus, a description of education law in Palestine without an accompanying description of its patchwork application would overlook the distinct features of the situation, namely fragmentation and its contribution to the weakening of legal protections for education, among other social and economic activities.

INSTITUTIONAL ISSUES

The fragmented nature of legal jurisdiction and educational provision is a defining characteristic of the prolonged occupation of the Palestinian territories. Despite this many hundreds of thousands of school children successfully receive a full-time education enabling them to study further and achieve a bachelor's degree or higher. The difficulties caused by occupation and fragmentation should not be allowed to eclipse the educational success story which has developed since 1994 at the inception of the fully Palestinian education system. This section describes the educational system and some of the characteristics of education in Palestine.

School System

Pre-school education or kindergarten stage—Early childhood education is provided to children between four and six years old.

Basic (or primary) education—This level, which includes grades 1–10, is divided into two stages: lower primary stage from first grade to fourth grade, and upper primary stage from the fifth grade to the tenth grade.

Secondary education—This level of academic education covers grades 11–12. There are three educational streams: humanities, sciences, and vocational education. The latter has five fields: commerce, agriculture, industry, tourism, and religion. Learners follow their choice of stream, depending on availability. After completion of these grades, students sit for the general secondary school examinations (*tawjihi*) which enables them to apply to institutions of higher learning.

Higher education—Students who pass their *tawjihi* can apply for higher learning courses leading to a diploma, a teaching qualification or Bachelor's degree. Foundation courses are also available for students who did not meet the entry requirements for some courses. Higher degrees and diplomas are also available.

Compulsory Attendance

Compulsory education aims to emphasize that neither parents nor guardians or the government have the right to view child education as if it were optional. It is well provided for in the legal framework. Basic education is compulsory and free. According to the Child Law, Article 37(1)(b) states: "Education is compulsory until the completion of the basic education stage." The Amended Basic Law stipulates that compulsory education shall cover primary education only. Article 10 of the Jordanian Education Law stipulates that the compulsory stage "shall be for nine years and it shall begin after a pupil's completion of age six."

Neither kindergarten nor secondary education is compulsory by law in Palestine. Due to its increased financial obligations, MOEHE only has an indirect role in supervising kindergarten education: it awards registration licenses after meeting certain conditions. Local, national, and international institutions within the private and civil sector have a primary role in this stage of education. While generally considered optional, kindergarten attendance is required by some private schools, considering the early childhood education experiences of learners beneficial before entering their academic institutions.

Many children continue into the two years of secondary education even though it is not compulsory. Free secondary education in government schools is guaranteed in Article 37(1)(a) of the Child Law.

Funding for Public Education

Public education in Palestine is primarily government-funded by the Palestinian National Authority (PNA). A special budget is usually approved for government educational institutions. This budget covers school employees' salaries, cost of curriculum development, and school buildings, including all the furnishings and regular maintenance. Given this huge burden, the PNA has faced difficulties in meeting all its debts. It has also become unable to earmark and allocate enough funding for advancing education and sometimes cannot pay teachers' salaries. Article 14 of the Jordanian Education Law permits the collection and raising of donations for schools, in accordance with a special system, in order to support school activities. This is often in the form of a small school fee levied from most children at the beginning of a term.

Governing Boards

Consisting of forty-one administrative units, MOEHE is the primary institution in charge of education development in the country, supervising both government- and privately-run schools along with higher education institutions as well as those schools run by the United Nations Relief and Works Agency (UNRWA). This is in accordance with Article 24 of the Amended Basic Law of 2003 which stipulates:

2. The PNA shall be in charge of all education in all its stages and it shall supervise all its institutions and raise their performance levels.
3. The law shall guarantee the independence of universities and higher education colleges and scientific research centres. It shall also protect freedom of scientific research, as well as literary, cultural, and artistic creativity. The PNA shall work to encourage and help these institutions.
4. Private schools and other academic institutions shall adopt the curricula approved by the PNA and shall be subjected to its supervision.

The PNA runs and finances the majority of basic and secondary schools in most of the West Bank and the Gaza Strip, with the exception of East Jerusalem, as discussed earlier. It takes responsibility for the development of the curriculum and teaching materials through its Curriculum Development Centre, under MOEHE. The Council for Higher Education facilitates the development and enactment of rules within each university.

To best align with international academic standards, an Accreditation and Quality Assurance Commission, also under MOEHE, oversees accreditation criteria and assessment procedures in institutions and programs of higher education. Technical and Vocational Education Training in Palestine is coordinated through a variety of agencies, including MOEHE, the Ministry of Labour, the Ministry of Social Affairs, UNRWA, and the private sectors and relevant NGOs.

Finally, adult education is facilitated by MOEHE, along with the following agencies, Ministry of Labour, Ministry of Social Affairs, Ministry of Women Affairs, participating universities, and local and international NGOs and women's organizations. Perceived as a social responsibility, adult education focuses on eradication of illiteracy, women's education, decreasing dropout rates, and on provision of vocational skills and training to workers.

Differences Between Public and Non-Public Schools

While both government and nongovernment schools adopt the curricula approved by the MOEHE in Palestine, there are a differences between the two types of schools. The primary difference between the two kinds of school lies in their supervision and sources of finance.

Government schools are directed by the MOEHE and financed by the PNA in all aspects, with a special item in the government budget allocated for their finance. Nongovernment, schools, on the other hand, are under the general supervision of the ministry, but are classified as private institutions and have their own administration. The schools are managed and funded by independent bodies, charitable societies, religious communities and individuals, with their own independent administrations. Officials in these schools are expected to inform the MOEHE about grants, donations, and assistance they receive from foreign sources in accordance with Article 70 of the Jordanian Education Law.

Under Article 24 of the Amended Basic Law, education in government schools is free while in nongovernment schools, tuition fees can be charged and specified by the individual school's authorities, but under the supervision of MOEHE. Further, while nongovernment schools may be shut down in case of violating effective laws and regulations, government schools may not be closed because they are public facilities serving the majority of students in Palestine.

In addition to private schools, other nongovernment schools include those run by UNRWA located in refugee camps in the West Bank, the Gaza Strip, and East Jerusalem. They include schools offering primary education from grade 1 to 9 and various post-secondary institutions which offer teaching or vocational education. As mentioned earlier, while MOEHE and UNRWA coordinate closely on many matters, MOEHE does not have full oversight of these schools.

Safety, Liability, and Negligence Issues

The inclusion of fragile indicators to monitor the disruption and violence of the occupation regime in MOEHE's annual monitoring framework was discussed earlier (MOEHE, 2014). Other safety measures at schools are in place and are thought to have a positive impact on the psychological well-being of both students and teachers. This leads to progress of the academic process in line with the expected outcomes. In its endeavor to make educational institutions enjoy the highest standards of safety, the MOEHE publishes annual guidelines and instructions pertinent to safety and responsibility with the aim of maintaining safety at schools for school children. These materials include standards for sanitary and hygiene conditions, infrastructure, roads, and health.

TEACHER RIGHTS

Like other countries, Palestine recognizes teachers as the foundation of the educational process. Yet despite that, there is no unified system to organize the work of teachers and regulate their rights. The rights of teachers are thus ambiguous and scattered broadly across the Palestinian legal system.

It is important to note that the Civil Service Law covers only government-run institutions, while public and private universities have their own specific regulations protecting faculty members. The above-mentioned ambiguity stems both from a lack of clarity in the existing regulations and the narrow nature of these regulations, especially when compared to higher education laws, relevant standards, and policies in other countries. When it comes to sabbatical leave, for instance, universities have their own regulations, selection processes and eligibility criteria which are not sufficiently clear, often resulting in a random applicant selection process.

Freedom of Speech

The Basic Law, which guarantee freedom of opinion and self-expression, encourages academic research. It also guarantees higher education institutions their independence while protecting freedom of academic research, literary creativity, and their encouragement and support.

At the end of 1994, the late president Yasser Arafat issued a presidential decree for the establishment of an independent monitoring body for human rights in the country—the Independent Commission for Human Rights. One of the aspects the commission was to observe was the freedom of speech. This provided an additional layer of observance of the existing Publication and Copyright Law which guarantees freedom of opinion and self-expression of every citizen and the freedom to access, publish, and exchange and comment on information. However, some articles appending the law had a restricting clauses which did not give persons all of their rights to freedom of opinion and self-expression.

The Jordanian Education Law regulates the work of primary public educational institutions. Article 5 of the law stipulates that the work of the MOEHE shall include the promotion of academic research, publication of its findings, sponsorship of talented people, and encouraging them to publish their intellectual work. Despite these protections, though, one cannot totally prevent the encroachments on the rights to public and academic freedom of expression from political, cultural, religious sources, and from the Israeli occupation.

In general, universities and schools are subject to the prevailing political conditions. Very often presidents and principals, respectively, are appointed with the strong influence of the state power. This is true in the Arab World in general and in Palestine to some extent. Therefore, institutions and their employees are run, as a general principle, based on the policies of the governing authority in the country. Pursuant to the Independent Commission for Human Rights (ICHR, 2014), the right of the opinion and self-expression in Palestine has been subjected to a number of violations by security organs in 2014.

Opinions or academic classifications which contravene commonly espoused religious or cultural beliefs could face harsh attacks from employees at academic institutions or from society in general. If such opinions are considered to be in conflict with Palestinian values and morals, according to Article 3 of Publishing and Copyright Law, an enforcement of a censorship or a ban may occur. These opinions or statements, in some cases, could also be considered crimes because they may be perceived to be insults to religious feelings. This is a crime which could lead to a three-month imprisonment for the writer.

The Amended Basic Law Article 4(2), states that, "The principles of Islamic shari'a shall be a principal source of legislation" which emphasizes a close alignment of Palestinian law with that of the prevailing religion. The Islamic religious curriculum is the official one in public schools. The Jordanian Education Law requires private schools to give Islamic education classes to Muslim pupils. The other school subjects, such as history and science, take religious principles into account and should not contravene or violate them.

Accordingly, one can say that private and public schools in Palestine, which have a religious orientation, limit teachers' freedom of expression and opinion about Palestinian religious and historical heritage. People of other faiths who also live in Palestine do have freedom of religious practice guaranteed by the Amended Basic Law, Article 18.

Finally, academic freedoms in Palestine have been significantly affected by the continuation of the Israeli occupation and its severe measures. The Israeli occupation authorities practice a collective punishment policy against the Palestinian civilian population in both the West Bank and the Gaza Strip, thus harming academic life in educational institutions. Israeli military measures include the attacks on the Gaza Strip, closure of towns and villages in the West Bank, and the prevention of students and teachers from having access to their schools or universities. This is in addition to the harassment, arrest, and detention of students and scholars.

Freedom of Religion

The Basic Law stipulates that freedom of belief, worship, and practice of religious rituals shall be guaranteed. Further, Article 9 bars discrimination on the basis of religion. The rules and criteria for appointment of teachers in public institutions, whether schools or higher educational institutions, contain no provisions discriminating on the basis of religion or belief. Moreover, the Labor Law, which applies to teachers in the private sector, stipulates that work shall be the right of every citizen without any type of discrimination. This implicitly includes nondiscrimination on the basis of religion or belief.

These provisions are in harmony with Article 18 of the International Covenant on Civil and Political Rights, to which Palestine acceded in 2014. They have also been emphasized in the Palestinian Independence Declaration. Nevertheless, these articles fall short of the Declaration of United Nations Assembly Resolution 36/55 of 1981 which calls for elimination of all forms of intolerance and discrimination on the basis of religious and belief.

Freedom of Association

The Basic Law stipulates that the right to form and establish labor unions shall be guaranteed for all. The Labor Law reiterates this right. Article 57 stipulates that private institutions, including those in the education sector, shall have the freedom to practice union work. Article 2(1) of the Civil Service Law also guarantees government employees and local authorities the freedom to exercise this right. In addition, the Basic Law and Labor Law provide for the right of workers to engage in strikes.

In spite of all this, there is no single unified law in the West Bank regulating union work in terms of establishing, registering, and dissolving unions. It is true that the Labor Law addresses some labor union issues such as the settlement of labor disputes, collective negotiations, strikes, and closures, but they are not sufficient. As a result, this has created a vacuum in legislative foundations and rules to guarantee union freedoms while regulating union work. At present, each professional union or syndicate has its own regulatory framework.

There are two teachers' unions in Palestine. The first, the Palestinian Teachers' Union, includes all employees in public schools. The second, the Federation of Unions of Palestinian Universities, includes all of the independent unions of universities. The Federation plays a key role in defending and protecting employees' rights.

For example, in 2011, the Federation represented university employees to MOEHE on a variety of grievances when they exercised their right to strike in addition to their right to demonstrate. The employees were able to gain both a salary increase and a fixed currency exchange rate for the currency in which their salaries were to be paid.

Most recently, in early 2016, teachers engaged in a month-long strike, asking for salary raises in keeping with inflation and a number of previously unmet requests, including permission to elect their own association body whose members would represent them more appropriately than the Teachers' Union. As a result, the government promised to pay teachers back pay in four installments and provide a 10 percent pay rise in the following years.

Numerous challenges face the work of the unions. One challenge is absence of union independence and the authoritarianism practiced by political parties and movements. Union work is directed and controlled by political parties in line with their political and party agendas. Moreover, union labor movement in Palestine is influenced by the PNA. One aspect of this containment is appointment of some union leaders in high-ranking government positions and providing them with government privileges such as paying them salaries and renting offices for them.

Pertaining to the teachers' participation in political parties, Article 25 of the Jordanian Education Law bars teachers from joining parties or practicing any party activity within the educational institution or outside of it. The purpose of this is to keep teachers independent and neutral in education, separating it from politics in any form. This law applies only to teachers in primary and secondary schools. The Higher Education Law of 1998 allows employees of higher education institutions to join political parties and practice party activities or participate in events in accordance with the internal policies of their institutions.

Other Constitutional Issues

The Basic Law Article 9 stipulates that "all Palestinians shall be equal before the law and the judiciary, without any distinction based upon race, sex, colour, religion, political opinion or disability." Article 26(4) stipulates that assuming public office or a public position is on the basis of equal opportunity. The Labor Law bans discrimination regardless of its form or type. Pertaining specifically to education, no law refers theoretically to discrimination of any sort or form.

Palestinian law explicitly addresses discrimination on the basis of gender. In 2014, the PNA acceded to the Convention on the Elimination of All Forms of Discrimination Against Women. Article 11 of this convention stipulates that "States Parties shall take all appropriate measures to eliminate discrimination against women in the field of employment."

In 2008, the Palestinian Cabinet established the National Commission for Women's Rights. The general aim of this commission was to foster and reinforce the principle of the rule of law, to be fair to women, and to improve institutional mechanisms for female victims of violence to access their rights on the basis of equal opportunity.

The Labor Law, in Article 100, bars any discrimination between men and women. In addition, women who work in private educational institutions are entitled to a variety of rights such as maternity leave, to leave without pay, to look after their children, and/or to accompany their spouses. However, such rights and privileges are not exercised and enjoyed by women working in public educational institutions; these women are governed by the Civil Service Law rather than the Labor Law which does not spell out such rights and special privileges.

Palestinian law addresses discrimination on the basis of disability in employment. In addition to the Basic Law, the Law of the Rights of the Disabled No. 4 of 1999 obliges the government and the nongovernmental institutions to ensure that at least 5 percent of their workforces must be people with disabilities. The Labor Law, in Article 13, also obliges the business owners to ensure that at least 5 percent of all of their employees are disabled.

Article 23 of the Civil Service Law of 1998 stipulates that it is possible to appoint blind persons or those with physical disabilities unless their impairments prevents them from performing the work they are assigned. In spite of these legal protections, there are still shortcomings in the extent of enforcing these laws due to the lack of a strong government follow up and control to check businesses' compliance with this law and respect of these rights.

STUDENT RIGHTS

In Palestine, students are not routinely made aware of a wide range of rights and protections because they have not been outlined in appropriate guidelines or protocols. There are documents in which academic obligations, rules, and regulations are specified. Additionally, a few documents address a narrow scope of student rights. However, they seem to resemble a list of "Dos" and

"Don'ts" highlighting potential disciplinary actions as a result of behavior offenses, rather than display what rights and protections they should have such as against being wrongfully punished or ways in which to exercise their liberties.

Admissions and Freedom from Discrimination

It has been noted that every child enjoys the right to education without discrimination. Also, every child is guaranteed a place in school. The net enrollment rate at the age of six is 98 percent, 97 percent for boys and 99 percent for girls, and is 100 percent at age seven (MOEHE, 2014). Nevertheless, daily practices still show clear societal gaps. For example, the rate at which children drop out of school is increasing, with as many as 3.5 percent leaving secondary school before completing. These rates are attributed to a lack of schools close to where learners live, the need for them to earn for their households or to do housework, and/or cost of transportation to and from school.

Some ex-detainees whose education was interrupted during their periods of incarceration in Israeli prison have difficulty completing their education. Although services are available for non-formal classes, many young ex-detainees have difficulty adjusting to expected scholastic performance.

Due Process Rights when Subject to Dismissal

Students' rights are embodied in the receipt of fair treatment when they are subject to disciplinary actions resulting from offences at school. Article 13 of the Jordanian Education Law emphasizes that pupils shall not be expelled from school before completion of the tenth grade. Exceptions to this rule are those who are mentally or physically ill.

With respect to students' behavior and attendance guidelines, MOEHE places great emphasis on good manners and regular attendance at school given their importance in the education of school pupils and their personal development. To these two ends, MOEHE has introduced a school disciplinary system to both public and nongovernment schools. The system is based on the general public Education Law, the Child Law, the Civil Service Law, as well as the guidelines and instructions issued by MOEHE. These legal instruments guarantee the right of protection and the right to education in safe and motivating environments away from fear and terror. Teachers also have the right to work in safe environments.

At the same time, MOEHE promotes desirable practices in schools as a means and a condition for efficient learning. MOEHE further attempts to provide and develop effective school systems which maintain discipline and put in place measures to check on school discipline problems in a cooperative participatory social framework. This contributes to a genuine interest in creating a humane environment for the pupils while upholding their right for dignity of life, growth, learning, respect, and consideration of their individual differences.

Violence in schools is increasing. A 2011 study on violence in the Palestinian society found that 20 percent of school students, aged twelve to seventeen, were subjected to psychological violence at school; another 20 percent were subjected to physical violence at the hands of their teachers (PCBS, 2011). About 15 percent of students said that they were witnesses of violence practiced by their peers. It is proposed that some teachers believe the use of violence is a socially acceptable means to discipline students' behaviors and improve their academic achievement.

Another challenge is the lack of a concrete monitoring system of problems at schools. Overcrowdedness of schools and classrooms, coupled with the absence of mechanisms of communication and dialogue between and among teachers, students, and families are all claimed to be further reasons for teachers' use of physical discipline in classes. Additionally, it is claimed that students' poor awareness of school rules and regulations may lead to the use of violent disciplinary measures.

In case of deviant behavior, such as sexual harassment, offenses are considered of the third degree and may receive tougher penalties. However, no cases on this issue have yet been brought for judicial review.

Freedom of Religion

Students have the freedom to practice their religious beliefs through prayer and dress as well as to exercise their freedom of expression and opinion in accordance with legal provision discussed earlier and in concordance with notions of public order and public manners. Paradoxically, though, while the school disciplinary system allows failure to wear a school uniform to be considered a punishable offence, this strict dress code contradicts the freedom of expression laid out in the Basic Law.

Students with Special Needs

The Law for the rights of the Disabled No. 4 of 1999 provides all persons with special needs equal opportunities for education. Even so, parents tend to send their male, rather than their female, children with special needs to school. This is an explicit violation of the right to education of female children with special needs.

The executive authorities have failed to set up necessary programs and plans, particularly for the deaf, to include children with special needs in public educational institutions. The overwhelming majority of children with special needs receive education in special institutions isolated from their local communities. This maintains the gap between children with special needs and their peers. Moreover, many families resist sending their children of either sex to educational institutions for a variety reasons, including financial. A shortage of places and suitable environments that foster inclusive education presents additional problems. Finally, there is a lack of a mechanism to oblige families to send their children with special needs to educational institutions.

EMERGING ISSUES

Technology

Since its establishment, the MOEHE has prioritized curriculum development as a strategic goal. It has taken scientific and technological progress into consideration by introducing Technology and Information Technology (IT) as a compulsory subject in grades 5–12. The promotion of technology in education is a major pillar of MOEHE's third strategic plan for educational development (2014–2019) (MOEHE, 2014). The major challenges to be overcome are the minimal use of existing facilities, shortfalls in teachers' competence to use or promote technology and a lack of a coherent IT strategy across the curriculum.

Curricular Development

Jordanian Education Law regulates issues pertinent to school curricula published by MOEHE. This law calls for the creation of a committee to develop curricula and textbooks along with a dedicated ministry department to undertake studies and scientific research while also supervising curricular issues. However, this law does not place restrictions on the nature or content of the curricula.

At the beginning of its work, MOEHE had to reconcile the existence of two different curricula in the West Bank and the Gaza Strip. The Jordanian curriculum was used in the West Bank while the Egyptian curriculum was used in the Gaza Strip. One of the priorities of the ministry at the time was to develop a Palestinian curriculum to meet the needs of pupils and unify the Palestinian educational system in the West Bank and the Gaza Strip. After a long and contentious process, the new curriculum was completed and progressively introduced into schools in 2000.

The new curriculum has been criticized for being academically traditional and containing a great deal of information emphasizing facts and knowledge. It is thought to lack contemporary necessary skills, such as critical thinking, problem solving, decision making, exploration, and research.

Standards in *Tawjihi*

Despite being a non-compulsory stage, many children continue into the two years of secondary education. These two years culminate in the general secondary examination—*tawjihi*. The examination covers all the subjects taken by the students following one of the three streams, testing their knowledge. The results of this examination are taken as the single most important indicator of a student's ability to progress to the next academic stage. It is seen as a life-changing examination, a stressful process for both students and their families.

The examination focuses on reading comprehension and relies on memorization. Methods for ensuring similar standards of performance receive equivalent scores year-on-year are not clearly defined or reported. Recently, Sabri Saidam, the Minister for Education and Higher Education, proposed reforms to *tawjihi* in order to revolutionize education in Palestine by inviting more creative and interactive approaches to teaching and learning.

CONCLUSION

The scene outside a typical school in Palestine at the end of a school day differs little to that outside any other school around the world. Children laden with backpacks are dashing for the school buses, teachers are packing up their materials for evenings of marking, and the premises are being swept and prepared for the next day. The form and function of school life are in common with anywhere else.

What characterizes education in Palestine is not simply a matter of underfunding, cultural preferences, and the slow progress of development, though they all contribute. Rather education is characterized by the influence of the constricting and fragmenting nature of the military occupation. The commentator is like a pin-ball focusing on the general characteristics of education—citing legal protections, quoting population statistics and averages—and then on the peculiarities—drilling into the margins and the less observed. At all levels, the reach of the occupation is unmistakable.

The development and promulgation of legislation is interrupted. The freezing of the Palestinian Legislative Council has driven the two authorities, in the West Bank and in the Gaza Strip, to issue separate legal protections. Further, while the unification of the two territories is disputed, no single unified education law exists. Efforts to streamline and unify protections for education should be considered. Palestine's accession in 2014 to various international human rights treaties offers established and recognized sources of normative standards for education and other entitlements associated with it.

The division of the Palestinian territory is not simply between the West Bank and Gaza Strip, but between eleven separately defined spaces. The regime of the Israeli occupation has brought about the physical fragmentation of the territory and population. The Oslo Accords contributed to the further fragmentation of the West Bank into Areas A, B, and C. Despite being conferred authority for education in Palestinian territory, the Palestinian National Authority does not have full legal jurisdiction over it all.

The Ministry of Education and Higher Education accepts its obligations for the education of the children in all divisions of Palestine. Yet taking responsibility in areas where it does not have civil or security control places it in an impossible position. The Ministry cannot be held to account for the actions of the Israeli military but cannot meet all its obligations because of its presence. If the PNA did not accept its responsibilities for the education of children in Area C, say, it would not only renege on its obligations, but also deny its claim on the territory. Yet in accepting its responsibilities, the PNA has to carry, in addition to the normal costs of education, the triple costs of occupation: the cost of vigilance and security; the cost of disruption, whether it is psychological or material; and the cost of repair and rehabilitation.

NOTES

1. It is a pleasure to thank those who helped us make this chapter possible, Irina Karic, Noor Adas, Mohammad Abushihahab, Reem Sawafta, and Tamer Abu Aisheh.

2. *Abu Libdeh et al. v. Minister of Education et al.* High Court of Justice (2008) 5373/08.

3. *Muhammad Farahat & Others v. Israeli Prison Service*, Tel Aviv District Court (1997) petition no. 97/400.

4. Military Order 1651 (2009) combined and replaced a variety of military orders covering security provisions and judicial and detention procedures while reiterating the age categories applied to Palestinians arrested in the West Bank: a child is up to the age of twelve; a juvenile is aged twelve or thirteen; a young adult is aged fourteen or fifteen; an adult is sixteen and older. See No Legal Frontiers (2014).

REFERENCES

Addameer (2010). *The right of child prisoners to education.* Retrieved May 22, 2014, from http://www.addameer.org/files/Reports/addameer-report-the-right-of-child-prisoners-to-education-october-2010-en.pdf.

———. (2014). *General briefing: Palestinian political prisoners in Israeli prisons.* Retrieved March 5, 2014, from http://www.addameer.org/etemplate.php?id=359.

———. (2016). *Statistics for February 2016.* Retrieved February 11, 2016, from http://www.addameer.org/statistics.

B'Tselem—The Israeli Information Centre for Human Rights in the occupied territories (2013). *Acting the landlord: Israel's policy in Area C, the West Bank.* Retrieved August 27, 2013, from http://www.btselem.org/publications/201306_area_c.

———. (2014). *The scope of Israeli control in the Gaza Strip.* Retrieved November 25, 2015, from http://www.btselem.org/gaza_strip/gaza_status.

———. (2015a). *Statistics on settlements and settler population.* Retrieved March 29, 2016, from http://www.btselem.org/settlements/statistics.

———. (2015b). *East Jerusalem* Retrieved March 29, 2016, from http://www.btselem.org/jerusalem.

———. (2015c). *Hebron City Centre—Updates.* Retrieved November 25, 2015, from http://www.btselem.org/ota?tid=155.

Cavanaugh, K. (2007). "The Israeli military court system in the West Bank and Gaza." *Journal of Conflict & Security Law*, 12(2), 197–222.

Civic Coalition for Defending the Palestinians' Rights in Jerusalem (2008). *Education in Jerusalem: Current situation and challenges ahead in the lack of a unified educational authority.* Retrieved November 25, 2015, from http://civiccoalition-jerusalem.org/human-rights-resources/publications/reports/education-jerusalem-current-situation-and-challenges-ahe.

Defense for Children International—Palestine Section [DCI/PS] (2015). *Military Detention.* Retrieved November 22, 2015, from http://www.dci-palestine.org/issues_military_detention.

Dinstein, Y. (2009). *The international law of belligerent occupation.* Cambridge: Cambridge University Press.

Hasson, N. (2012). "A surprising process of 'Israelization' is taking place among Palestinians in East Jerusalem." *Haaretz newspaper 29 December 2012.* Retrieved February 5, 2014, from http://www.haaretz.com/weekend/magazine/a-surprising-process-of-israelization-is-taking-place-among-palestinians-in-east-jerusalem.premium-1.490367.

Independent Commission for Human Rights [ICHR] (2014). *Status of Human Rights in Palestine—Twentieth Annual Report—Executive Summary.* Retrieved March 30, 2016, from http://www.ichr.ps/en/2/6/1360/ICHR.

International Court of Justice (2004). *Legal consequences of the construction of a wall in the occupied Palestinian territory (Advisory opinion) [2004] ICJ Rep 136.* Retrieved February 21, 2012, from http://www.icj-cij.org/docket/files/131/1671.pdf.

Ir Amim and Association for Civil Rights in Israel [ACRI] (2012). *Failed grade—East Jerusalem's failing education system.* Retrieved August 8, 2013, from http://www.acri.org.il/en/2012/08/28/ej-education-report2012/.

Ministry of Education and Higher Education [MOEHE] (2013). *Education statistical yearbook for scholastic year 2012/13.* Retrieved October 2, 2014, from http://www.moehe.gov.ps/Uploads/admin/Statistical%20Book%20final.pdf.

——— (2014). *Education Development Strategic Plan 2014–2019—A learning nation.* Retrieved November 25, 2015, from http://www.moehe.gov.ps/en/Plans-Strategies/Education-Dev-Strategic-Plan-EDSP/2014.

Nicolai, S. (2007). *Fragmented foundations: Education and chronic crisis in the Occupied Palestinian Territory.* Paris: UNESCO-International Institute for Educational Planning and London: Save the Children UK. Retrieved January 25, 2010, from http://unesdoc.unesco.org/images/0015/001502/150260e.pdf.

No Legal Frontiers (2014). *Order regarding security provisions, No. 1651.* Retrieved March 13, 2014, from http://nolegalfrontiers.org/en/military-orders/mil01.

Palestinian Central Bureau of Statistics [PCBS] (2015). *Palestinians at the end of 2015.* Retrieved March 30, 2016, from http://www.pcbs.gov.ps/pcbs_2012/Publications.aspx.

———. (2011). *Violence survey in the Palestinian society, 2011. Main findings.* Retrieved March 30, 2016, from http://www.pcbs.gov.ps/PCBS-Metadata-en-v4.2/index.php/catalog/141/study-description.

Palestinian Centre for Human Rights (2013). *PNGO and Palestinian human rights organisations call for the end to application to Education Law, halt to the enactment of unnecessary legislation in light of division.* Retrieved November, 25, 2015, from http://www.pchrgaza.org/portal/en/index.php?option=com_content&view=article&id=9408:pngo-and-palestinian-human-rights-organisations-call-for-end-to-application-of-education-law-halt-to-the-enactment-of-unnecessary-legislation-in-light-of-division&catid=36:pchrpressreleases&Itemid=194.

Palestinian National Authority (PNA). (2010). *The Palestinian National Authority report on the implementation of the Convention on the Rights of the Child in the occupied Palestinian territory.* Retrieved March 26, 2012, from http://www.savethechildren.org.uk/resources/

online-library/the-palestinian-national-authority-report-on-the-implementation-of-the-convention-on-the-rights-of-the-child-in-the-occupied-palestinian-territory.

Shalhoub-Kevorkian, N. (2008). The gendered nature of education under siege: A Palestinian feminist perspective. *International Journal of Lifelong Education*, 27(2), 179–200.

United Nations General Assembly (2012). *Status of Palestine in the United Nations*. Sixty-seventh session. 26 November 2012. A/67/L.28.

———. (2013). *Peaceful settlement of the question of Palestine*. Sixty-eighth session. 30 January 2014. A/RES/68/15.

United Nations General Assembly and Security Council (2015). *Children and Armed Conflict—Report to the Secretary General*. Sixty-ninth session of the General Assembly. Sixty-ninth year of the Security Council. 5 June 2015. Agenda Item 64. A/69/926 and S/2015/409.

United Nations Human Rights Council (2008). *Human rights situation in Palestine and other occupied Arab territories—Human rights violations emanating from Israeli military attacks and incursions in the Occupied Palestinian Territory, particularly the recent ones in the occupied Gaza Strip*. Eighth session. 6 June 2008. A/HRC/8/17.

———. (2013). *Report of the Special Rapporteur on the situation of human rights in the Palestinian territories occupied since 1967, Richard Falk*. Twenty-third session. 3 June 2013. A/HRC/23/21.

United Nations Office for the Coordination of Humanitarian Affairs for the occupied Palestinian territories [UN-OCHA] (2011a). *Barrier Update—Seven years after the advisory opinion of the International Court of Justice: Impact of the barrier in the Jerusalem area*. Retrieved August 27, 2013, from http://www.ochaopt.org/documents/ocha_opt_barrier_update_july_2011_english.pdf.

———. (2011b). *Special focus: Displacement and insecurity in Areas C of the West Bank*. Retrieved October 3, 2014, from http://www.ochaopt.org/documents/ocha_opt_area_c_report_august_2011_english.pdf.

———. (2013). *The humanitarian impact of Israeli settlements on Hebron City*. Retrieved March 29, 2016, from https://www.ochaopt.org/results.aspx?id=4771279.

———. (2014). Area C of the West Bank: Key humanitarian concerns. Retrieved October 7, 2015, from http://www.ochaopt.org/results.aspx?id=4771485.

United Nations Relief and Works Agency for Palestinian Refugees in the Near East [UNRWA] (2014). *Where we work*. Retrieved February, 2, 2014, from http://www.unrwa.org/where-we-work.

Chapter Four

Republic of Korea

Jang Wan Ko, Sheena Choi,
and Hyowon Park

INTRODUCTION

Education is viewed as one of the fundamental values of Republic of Korea (henceforth, referred to as "South Korea" or "Korea") where academic success is often a source of pride for families and the main engine of social mobility. As such, the majority of South Koreans places singular importance on education; this is often referred to as "education fever" (Seth 2002).

South Korea ranks among the highest OECD (Organization for Economic Cooperation and Development) countries in educational attainment; about 98 percent of Korean students finish secondary education while 65 percent of Koreans between the ages of twenty-five and thirty-four have attained tertiary education (Clark & Park, 2013). This is a remarkable development insofar as South Korea has a relatively short history of modern education.

This chapter is organized in the following manner: legal statutes underpinning primary and secondary education; institutional issues as examined through historical review of compulsory attendance, funding for public education, governing boards, and different types of public and non-public schools. The chapter then examines faculty rights to due process in hiring, promotion, tenure, and dismissal; freedom of speech; freedom of religion; and freedom of association with regard to organizing and operating unions.

Next, the chapter examines student rights as to admission processes and freedom from discrimination based on race, gender, disability, or religion; due process rights when subjected to dismissal for academic and or disciplinary infractions; search and seizure/drug testing; freedom of religion; freedom of speech; and students with special needs. In addition, the chapter deals with emerging issues in Korean education such as school violence, character education, and preschool programs known as Nuri.

LEGAL SOURCES OF PRIMARY AND SECONDARY EDUCATION

Education Law in South Korea is governed primarily by three major acts: The Framework Act on Education, the Elementary and Secondary Education Act (ESEA), and the Higher Education Act, a statute beyond the scope of this chapter. The Framework Act on Education aims to provide for the rights and duties of citizens along with the obligations of the state and local governments on education; it also prescribes the educational system and fundamental subjects for its operation.

Generally, the Framework Act addresses the principle of education, the right to learn, equal opportunity of education, educational independence, educational neutrality, educational finance, compulsory education, school education, social education, and the establishment of schools. The Elementary and Secondary Education Act (ESEA) addresses matters regarding the elementary and secondary education under the provisions of Article 9, School Education, of the Framework Act on Education.

Many laws and regulations are relevant to elementary and secondary education in South Korea. The key laws and regulations are the ESEA, the Enforcement Decree of the ESEA, the Public Education Officials Act, the Decree on the Appointment of Public Education Officials, the Private School Act, the Enforcement Decree of the Special Cases Concerning the Disclosure of Information by Education, and the Presidential Decree.

Another law, the Public Education Officials Act applies to the public education officials in respect of their qualifications, appointment, salary, study and training, status guarantee, and the like, taking into account the special character of their duties and responsibilities of serving the entire nation through education. The purpose of the Private School Act is to ensure the sound development of these schools by securing their independence and promoting their public characteristics in view of their special characteristics.

INSTITUTIONAL ISSUES

Compulsory Attendance

In accordance with the provisions of the Framework Act on Education (Article 8), the ESEA addresses mandatory education in the form of elementary and middle schools. According to the ESEA, the government shall provide mandatory education and take necessary actions for schooling; local governments must establish and operate elementary schools, middle schools, and special schools necessary to educate all persons subject to mandatory education in their jurisdictions (Article 12).

According to Article 13 of the Act, Duty to School Attendance, "All people shall send their children, whom they protect, to an elementary school from March 1st of the following year after their children become six years old to the end of February of the following year when their children become 12 years old." School attendance age may be between the ages of five to seven depending on students' physical, psychological, and intellectual conditions.

As to middle schools, the Act includes a similar provision. The Act mandates that "All people shall send their children . . . to a middle school for the period from the following year after their children graduate from elementary school to the end of February of the following year after their children become 15 years old," meaning that these students typically enter between the ages of fourteen and sixteen.

The idea of compulsory education in South Korea goes back to 1945, right after liberation. In 1948, when the first Korean Constitution was established, it included mandatory primary education. The first Education Act, established in 1949 in accordance with the Constitution, declared the necessity of mandatory education. Based on the Education Act, the mandatory primary education officially started in 1950.

Although the idea of perfect compulsory education was delayed due to the Korean War (1950–1953), the six-year Plan for Mandatory Education (1954–1959) was established right after the Korean War. As a result of the Plan, the number of elementary schools increased from 2,834 to 4,496 between 1945 and 1960, and the number of students increased by more than twice, from 1,366,685 to 3,622,685 during the same period (Ministry of Education, 2007).

In the development of Korean education, its most outstanding feature during the 1960s was its quantitative expansion in student population (Ministry of Education, 2007). The number of students increased by 59 percent, 149 percent, and 116 percent in elementary, middle, and high schools, respectively, between 1960 and 1970. While governmental policy heavily focused on the primary education in the 1950s, the number of students in middle schools also rapidly increased from 80,828 to 528,593 between 1945 and 1960. Insofar as elementary schools achieved almost 100 percent attendance in the late 1950s, 96.5 percent in 1959, compulsory education for middle school students became the focus in the 1960s.

The percentage of middle school attendance was 32.2 percent in 1960, a very low rate compared with that of elementary schools. Although the government tried to expand the middle school population, the attendance rate was not much improved and remained below 40 percent by 1965 (Lee et al.,

2009, p. 557). The unbalanced attendance rates caused social problems such as a large increase in private tutoring expenditure to prepare children for entrance examinations and extremely high competition for entrance into middle schools.

The government introduced a new policy to alleviate the problems caused by the middle school entrance examination in the late 1960s. In 1968, the government abolished the middle school entrance examination, instead introducing a system of student allocation in which primary school graduates were assigned to middle schools through a lottery system. With the elimination of the middle school entrance examination, the flow of students into and out of the middle school system greatly increased. As a result, the attendance rate increased to 53.3 percent in 1970, 74.0 percent in 1975, and 82.0 percent in 1985. Finally, the attendance rate reached over 91 percent in 1990 (Lee et al., 2009, p. 557).

Funding for Public and Religiously Affiliated Non-Public Schools

Funding for primary and secondary education is regulated by the Framework Act for Education, Education Tax Act, and Local Education Finance Subsidy Act. In 2016, primary and secondary education spent about 74.4 percent of all educational expenditure, while higher education spent 16.6 percent, and other categories including lifelong education spent the rest of the expenditures. Both national/public and private primary and secondary schools receive educational funding from the central government and local educational authorities (OECD, 2010).

National schools operate on personnel fees and operational costs subsidized by the Ministry of Education, which supervises and inspects the schools. National schools also draw expenses from facility costs and user fees. Public schools operate on operational expenses and facility costs subsidized by the Metropolitan/Provincial Offices of Education (MPOE), personnel fees covered by local governments, and user fees. Resources of the MPOEs primarily consist of the government's local education subsidy, support from the national treasury, and the offices' revenues.

Private schools, including those with religious affiliations, are basically financed by subsidies through local education authorities. The government has been subsidizing private schools since 1974 when the high school equalization policy was introduced. The policy applied to all, both national/public and private schools. With the exception of a portion of private schools composing a large part of their budgets with fund transfers from School Foundations, most private schools receive a considerable amount of financial support from the national treasury.

Recently, many different types of schools emerged: foreign language high schools (*Oegugeo Godeunghaggyo*), science and technology high schools (*Gwahak Godeunghaggyo*), international high schools (*Kugje Godeunghaggyo*), and self-financed private high schools (*Jaripyeong Sarip Godeunghaggyo*). Because self-financed private high schools receive no governmental subsidies, they charge very high tuition and fees to students and parents.

Aside from direct government general subsidies, schools can receive public subsidies by applying to become beneficiary institutions of various educational support programs provided by the central government and local educational authorities. Those financial support programs include the Project to Assist After-school Programs, Support Project to Designate Classrooms by Subject, Project to Support Schools with No Private Tutoring, and Project to Aid Target Schools in Need of Academic Ability Enhancement.

Governance

The Ministry of Education is the central government office overseeing the education sector. As for local authorities, there are sixteen Metropolitan/Provincial Offices of Education (MPOEs) located in seven major cities and nine provinces overseeing local educational administration. While the Ministry is responsible for establishing and implementing national policies for school education, MPOEs set up and implement policies for local school education and provide support for schools within their jurisdiction. At the regional level, local education offices exist under MPOEs to support schools.

Individual schools operate under the authority of their principals. In recent years, though, teachers and parents have been involved more deeply in school management through various school councils and committees. At the elementary and secondary school level, the most important committee is the School Operation Committee. The ESEA requires all schools including national, public or private elementary schools, middle schools, high schools, and special schools to establish and operate the School Operation Committees to enhance the autonomy of their operations and creatively conduct various educations suitable for local situations and characteristics (Article 31, Item 1).

The number of members for School Operation Committees shall be within the range of five to fifteen people taking school size into consideration. However, detailed information about the construction and operation of School Operation Committees is determined by other regulations based on the status of the schools. For example, the construction and operation of the committee at national schools is established by the presidential decree, but the construction and operation of the committees at public schools is established by the City/*Do* ordinances within the range set by the presidential decree. For private schools, matters on the makeup of the committees is determined by the presidential decree; other necessary matters on the operation thereof are established under the provisions of the Articles of the School Incorporation (Article 34).

The functions of the School Operation Committees at national or public schools are to deliberate on the following matters:

- the establishment or amendment of school charters and school rules;
- school budget plans or settlements of accounts;
- the operational methods of school education processes;
- selecting educational books, texts, and materials;
- items to be paid by students' parents such as school uniforms, training uniforms, graduation albums, and the like;
- educational and training activities after regular class time and/or during vacation periods;
- recommendations of invited teachers in accordance with the provisions of Article 31 (2) of the Public Education Officials Act;
- raising, operating, and using of school operation support funds;
- school meal plans;
- recommendations from the heads of schools among the special selections of college entrance;
- construction and operation of school athletic departments;
- suggestions and recommendations on school operations; and
- other items as determined by the Presidential Decree or City/*Do* ordinances.

The heads of private schools shall undergo the counseling of the School Operation Committee on matters addressed above except for matters on the recommendation of invited teachers. However, the committee shall provide advice to the matters on the establishment or amendment of school charters and rules only when it is requested by school corporations. In addition, the School Operation Committees shall deliberate on and determine the raising, operation, and use of school advancement funds.

Differences Between and Among Types of Public and Non-Public Schools

Various types of schools exist at the primary and secondary education levels. These schools include primary schools, civic schools, middle schools, higher citizenship training schools, civic high schools, general high schools, vocational and technical high schools, air and correspondence high schools, trade high schools, high schools affiliated to industrial firms, and special schools. In general, though, primary and secondary education is divided into primary schools, middle schools, high schools, and special schools.

The purpose of elementary schools is to provide basic education necessary for everyday life. Middle schools aim to provide middle education on the base of education which is provided from elementary schools; high schools aim to provide middle education or basic expert education on the base of education from middle schools. The purpose of special schools is to assist students who have physical, mental, or intellectual disabilities and are in need of special education, by providing them with education equivalent to primary, middle, and high schools and educating them on knowledge, skills, and social adaptation techniques necessary for practical everyday life.

At the high school level, various types of schools exist. The most common and popular type of high school is a general high school, which prepares students for higher education institutions (HEIs). Vocational high school is another common school form, for the people who plan to work right after high school graduation or who plan to go to junior colleges. Various types of professional high schools have been operated for years: foreign language high schools, science and technology high schools, and international high schools. These professional schools have their own purposes as the titles of schools imply and are for the talented students.

Recently, a new form of high school, self-financed private high schools, has emerged. While most high schools do not have power to select their own students because of the High School Equalization Policy, the self-financed private high schools along with other professional high schools can select their own students and charge very high tuition and fees to students and parents.

In addition, the ESEA addresses foreigner schools and alternative schools (Article 60). Foreigner schools are for the children of foreigners who have resided in Korea or children of Koreans who resided in foreign countries and returned to Korea. Alternative schools provide various types of educational experiences such as experiential education including field education, personality education, talent and aptitude development education for the students who stopped studying or intend to receive education that fits their individuality. Foreigner schools and alternative schools may integrate and operate the kindergarten, elementary, middle, and high school courses. Establishment and operations of foreigner schools including the establishment standards, curriculum, school years, and academic acknowledgments shall be determined by the presidential decree.

FACULTY RIGHTS

Due Process Rights in Hiring, Promotion and Tenure, and Dismissal

The appointment of teachers is described in the ESEA and the Public Education Officials Act. Public school teachers are considered public education officials who shall be appointed pursuant to their qualifications, results of reeducation, service records, and actual proof of other capabilities (Public Education Officials Act, Article 10). Basically, the appointment of new teachers is based on open screening tests; the presidential decree prescribes age requirements and qualifications necessary for performing their duties and other detailed information of the test including procedures, methods, and evaluation factors. Like students, teachers have the right to freedom from discrimination based on race, gender, disability, and/or religion.

For the Teacher's Employment Examination (*Kywon Imyong Gosa*), only candidates holding teachers' licenses can apply for this test. In order to have teachers' licenses, candidates must complete the teacher education programs in HEIs. There are three types of teacher education programs in general with HEIs offering one or more of them depending on their capabilities.

The most common approach for teacher candidates is to complete the subject-specific programs in the designated departments of their colleges or schools of education. The students can also take teacher-preparation courses required by the government and universities. Graduate colleges of education also offer regular programs for students who seek to become teachers and retraining programs for current teachers. The University of Education, a stand-alone institution for cultivating elementary teachers exclusively, also provides teacher education programs. Students who complete the teacher education programs in HEIs are awarded grade 2 teachers' licenses.

Since almost no hierarchy exists between teachers, there is no provision about the promotion of teachers in schools in the ESEA. Teacher positions consist of three levels, principals, assistant principals, and teachers. However, principals and assistant principals are considered as administrators. There are two types of teacher positions, grade 1 and grade 2, for regular teachers; there are other types of teachers such as expert counseling teachers, literature teachers, hygiene teachers, and nutrition teachers. Teachers who hold the grade 2 license initially can be promoted to grade 1 license teachers after three years of on-the-job experiences and following the completion of professional development training. For teachers with grade 1 licenses, they remain in their positions until retirement unless they want to become principals and assistant principals.

Recently, the government introduced a new position for teachers, the Master teacher (*Suseok kyosa*) system intended to support senior teachers who wish to remain in their classrooms rather than become administrators. Individuals with over fifteen years of teaching experience can apply for positions as Master teachers. Candidates should pass the screening tests consisting of three steps including document review, teaching ability and interview test, and an interview with peer teachers. After passing the test, Master teachers must take ninety-hour basic training courses before appointment. In addition, Master teachers should complete ninety-hour professional development courses every year.

The Public Education Officials Act establishes the guarantee of status for public education officials including teachers (Article 43). Public education officials are free from unjust interference affecting their special position or status, shall not be recommended to resign, and shall not be laid off, demoted, or discharged against their will except as a sentence for punishment, a disciplinary action, or other grounds prescribed by this Act. In addition, teachers cannot be arrested in schools without the consent of the heads of the school to which they belong except in the case of being caught flagrante delicto (Article 48). Teachers and other educational officials have a retirement age. The age limit of for public education officials is sixty-two; the retirement age for professors in HEIs is sixty-five years of age.

Freedom of Speech

Freedom of speech of school teachers is mainly related to Educational Neutrality. Other Acts including the national Constitution, the Framework Act on Education, and Private School Act address the political neutrality of education. For example, the Korean Constitution declares that "The status and political impartiality of public officials shall be guaranteed as prescribed by Act" (Article 7), and "Independence, professionalism and political impartiality of education and the autonomy of institutions of higher learning shall be guaranteed under the conditions as prescribed by Act" (Article 31).

The Framework Act on Education also addresses the educational neutrality, stating that "Education shall be operated to perform its functions according to the purpose of the education per se and it shall not be used as a tool for propagating any political, factional or individual biased views" (Article 6) and "School teachers shall not guide or instigate students for the purpose of supporting or opposing any particular political party or faction" (Article 14). Further, the Private School Act indicates that authorities may dismiss a teacher from office who "participates in a political movement, or refuses lectures and seminars in a group, or guides and agitates the students to support or to oppose a political party" (Article 58).

These Acts are intended to guarantee educational neutrality to protect students from the personal political views of teachers. Even so, critics argue that the legislation tends to limit freedom of speech by strongly emphasizing the "responsibility" of teachers, instead of viewing it as a "basic right" of citizens. In addition, the critics argue that the articles in the Framework Act on Education possibly are conflicted with the national Constitution.

Freedom of Religion

Article 20 of the national Constitution clearly provides for freedom of religion:

"(1) All citizens enjoy the freedom of religion. (2) No state religion may be recognized, and church and state are to be separated." However, the Framework Act on Education prohibits religious education in national and public schools, declaring that no school founded by the state or local governments shall conduct religious education on behalf of any particular religion. Private schools are free to teach religion.

In some cases, teachers have expressed their own views and insisted on particular religions, thereby causing problems in schools. For example, the Center for Student Rights in Cheonbook Province recommended a severe penalty for a history teacher in a public school who expressed and insisted on his religious perspectives in classes (Cheonbook Ilbo, 2015).

Freedom of Association

Freedom of association, especially to establish and operate teacher unions, has been a top issue in Korean education in recent decades. The first "Act on the Establishment, Operation, Etc., of Trade Unions for Teachers" was established in 1999. Based on the Act, which allows establishing associations or unions of teachers, the Korean Teachers and Education Workers Union was established in 1989 and granted legal status. Other teacher associations and unions were established in 1991.

Traditionally, the Korean Federation of Teachers' Association (KFTA) founded in 1949 was only a teacher association until the Korean Teachers and Education Workers Union (KTU) was established in 1989. The KTU has actively engaged in political events and it has raised many issues. The Act on the Establishment, Operation, of Trade Unions for Teachers especially targets teacher unions. According to the Act, teachers may establish trade unions at the special city, metropolitan city, province or special self-governing province levels or at the national levels (Article 4). However, trade unions for teachers are not allowed to participate in political activities (Article 3, Prohibition of Political Activities).

The representatives of trade union have the authority to bargain and conclude collective agreements over the improvement of the economic and social status of teachers, such as wages, working conditions, and welfare with the Minister of Education, the superintendent of the city and provincial office of education, or the person who establishes and operates a private school. In the case of private schools, persons who establish and maintain such schools shall participate in negotiations at the national level or at the city or provincial levels.

If two or more trade unions operate in the same school, they shall establish a single bargaining channel or representative to demand collective bargaining. In addition, if the parties engage in bargaining or conclude a collective agreement, they must negotiate in good faith, taking into consideration the opinion of the public and parents, and shall not abuse their authority. The presidential decree prescribes other matters concerning procedures for collective bargaining.

Trade unions and their members are prohibited from taking industrial actions, including strikes, work slowdowns, or other activities hindering normal business operations. Even so, if collective bargaining breaks down, either or both of the parties concerned may make requests for mediation to the National Labor Relations Commission. The commission has the authority to commence mediation without delay during which the parties shall participate in good faith.

STUDENT RIGHTS

The Admissions Process

Students have rights to enter elementary and middle schools as the ESEA requires. Students who graduated from elementary schools or are acknowledged as having equivalent academic achievement under the provisions of the relevant laws and regulations are eligible to enter middle schools. The heads of schools are responsible for determining enrollment, reenrollment, expulsion, change of school, transference and temporary absence of middle school students in accordance with school rules unless there are special regulations. Basically, the government uses drawing methods to assign new students to immediate upper levels of schools. The detailed process is described as follows (Article 68).

The admission process takes multiple steps. First, children who intend to enroll in middle schools must submit middle school assignment applications to the Middle School Drawing Management Committees to which their elementary schools belong. Second, the Superintendent of the Office of Education (SOE) through the approval of education committee selects the areas, school districts, middle school districts, and drawing methods. In this case relevant information should be announced. Third, the SOE places applicants for middle school by drawing in accordance with their areas and school districts. Further, students may be placed at schools in accordance with the middle school districts as prescribed by the SOE if the area is considerably inconvenient for commuting due to reasons such as distance and difficulty with transportation.

In the event of selecting middle schools by drawing, applicants for middle schools located in the areas as selected and announced by the SOE may choose and apply for more than two schools by the methods and procedures set by the SOE; the SOE may select, by drawing, all or part of the fixed number of the respective schools among the applicants. In order to execute drawings, Middle School Drawing Management Committees shall be placed in each school district under the SOE. Middle School Drawing Management Committees consist of five to seven members appointed by the SOE; necessary matters as to their constitutions and operation are established by the City/*Do* education rules.

Heads of school conducts enrollment screenings for high schools. In this case, for the fair management of enrollment screenings for high schools, the SOE establishes and announces, by March 31 of each year, the basic plan of enrollment screening to establish the basic matters on enrollment screening such as procedures and methods of screening.

In the event that the executor of enrollment screening for high schools intends to perform the enrollment screening, the executor should establish and announce the plan no later than three months before the execution date within the range of the enrollment screening basic plan. Regarding the application for enrollment screening process for high schools, students who intend to apply for high school enrollment screenings shall select one school in the area where its middle school is located and apply to the enrollment screening executor of the respective school.

Special cases exist regarding student recruitment. The heads of high schools may select students who attended middle schools besides the areas where the competent high schools are located within the range as selected through discussions between the enrollment screening executor and the Minister of Education. These schools include schools not receiving staff personnel expenses and curricular operations costs from the state or local self-governing bodies or schools exceeding the standards of corporation transference money as determined by the Minister of Education. In this case, the recruitment ratio is set in the range so that it does not damage the application principle of the enrollment screening.

Regarding enrollment screening methods, there is a two-term system based on the type of schools. Enrollment screening for the first-term schools such as professional and vocational high schools may be executed by methods reflecting practical examinations, aptitude tests, experiments, and interviews as part of the screening methods. Enrollment screening for second-term schools such as general high schools should be conducted by the middle-school life record, or other usable data where there is no school life record available, selection examination, or a method integrating both of the above.

The admission process and other school policies apply to all students without discrimination. Moreover, the ESEA addresses the process and policies for special populations such as the children of overseas Koreans, foreigners, and refugees of North Korea (Articles 19, 75, and 89). Put another way, students returning from foreign countries, foreign students, and the children of defectors from North Korea may apply to the schools in residential areas. In this case, the head of the school in the residential areas of the children may check their immigration and other related documents.

Disciplinary Due Process

A head of a school may discipline or otherwise guide students under the conditions as determined by the laws and regulations or school rules. Five types of student punishment are indicated in the Enforcement Decree of the ESEA, namely service in school, social service, completion of special programs, suspension, and expulsion from school (Article 31). When disciplining students, a head of a school shall undergo proper procedures such as giving the pupils and/or their parents opportunities to state their opinions before imposing punishments. Further, when imposing punishments, heads of school should use educational methods respectful of the students' character and apply the types of punishments step by step in accordance with the gravity of the reasons in order to give students opportunities to repent.

Expulsions from school apply to any students whose behavior is poor and who is deemed to be unable to improve, who is absent from school frequently without any justifiable reason, and who violates other school rules. However, students in the process of mandatory education such as elementary and middle schools shall not be expelled from schools (Article 18 of the ESEA). Before administering expulsions, heads of the schools may have the students study at home for periods of time. In it is necessary to expel students, the heads of schools shall provide career counseling to the pupils and guardians while making efforts to recommend other schools or vocational education training institutions.

Any students or their guardians objection to expulsions or other punishments may file objections with the City/*Do* Mediation Committee for Student Discipline or Student Punishment Settlement Committee (hereinafter Punishment Settlement Committee) within fifteen days of the date on which the disposition was determined or within ten days of the date on which they became aware of the disposition. In this case, the Punishment Settlement Committee shall consider the case and notify the parties of its decision within thirty days. Those who object to this decision may file for an administration trial within sixty days after receiving the notification.

Punishment Settlement Committees consist of not more than seven members including one chairperson. Members of this Committee are appointed by the Superintendent of the Office of Education from among those who meet the following qualifications:

- Two people among school inspectors, education inspectors, junior supervisors, education researchers or middle school teachers with more than fifteen years of teaching experience;
- Police officers who belong to the local stations of the competent areas;
- Person qualified as lawyers;
- Those with positions higher than assistant professor at colleges or researcher institutions;
- Parents of students at schools in the area under the jurisdiction of the Superintendent of the Office of Education or the representatives of non-profit private organizations related to education; and
- Counseling experts in youth related organizations or youth counseling institutions or psychiatrists of medical facilities.

Members serve two-year terms and can be reappointed for consecutive terms. Committee Heads are appointed by the Superintendent of the Office of Education and can both summon and chairperson meetings. When calling meetings, the chair shall notify members of the date, place, and subject of the meeting via letters or other modes of communication at least five days in advance. The committee must have a quorum of at least half of its registered members and must reach decision by a majority vote of those attending its meetings.

Other Student Rights

The major education laws such as the Framework Act on Education, the Elementary and Secondary Education Act, the Enforcement Decree of the ESEA and the Private School Act regulate only limited areas of student activities. These acts do not address such concerns as drug testing, freedom of religion of students, and freedom of speech of students. However, the ESEA notes that self-governing activities of students are encouraged and protected, specifying that basic matters on student organizations and their operations are set by school rules.

Students with Special Needs

The ESEA addresses special education. Under this law, special schools aim to provide education equivalent to elementary, middle, and high schools as well as knowledge and techniques necessary for everyday life and social adaptation education for those who need special education due to physical, mental, or intellectual disabilities (Article 55).

Schools lower than high schools may have special classes after obtaining the approval of competent offices for students needing special education. Special schools with high school courses may provide professional technical education to these students. In addition, the state and local self-governing bodies shall take necessary measures for integrated education such as preparing extra entrance procedures and courses when those needing special education want to receive education at schools equivalent to elementary, middle, and high schools (Article 59).

Students who completed courses equivalent to elementary, middle, and high school education at special schools or special classes are considered to have equal academic qualifications as those who graduated from regular schools. The ESEA also addresses the Education for Slow Learning Children, obligating state and local self-governing bodies to take necessary measures such as flexible operation of school days and academic curricula, as prescribed by the presidential decree, for students who are slow learners, have personality disorders, or other conditions requiring special education (Article 28).

EMERGING ISSUES

There are emerging Korean K–12 educational law issues: school violence, character education, and "Nuri" curricula for preschools. The issues are related to the Act on the Prevention, Countermeasures against Violence in Schools and Character Education Promotion Act, and Nuri Curriculum, respectively. The first two issues are somewhat related because one of the reasons for starting the discussion about the need for character education was the increase in school violence in elementary and high schools. On the other hand, Nuri curricula apply to students in kindergarten.

School Violence

On January 29, 2004, the Korean government enacted the Act on the Prevention and Countermeasures against Violence in Schools to eliminate school violence. Since then, the Act was amended seven times, mainly focusing on improving school violence prevention system. The amendments are primarily concentrated on expanding the types of forbidden school violence and strengthening the measures imposed on offenders (Moon & Kang, 2015).

The law defines school violence as "any activities that involve injury, assault, confinement, threat, kidnap, defamation, insult, coercion, sexual abuse, outcast, or providing violence information that causes any physical, mental, or property damages to students within and outside of school (The

Office of Legislation, 2016)." The purpose of the Act is "to prepare preventions and measures for school violence that foster students to sound individuals and secure students' right by protecting victims, guiding and educating offenders, and disputing conciliation between victims and offenders (The Office of Legislation, 2016)."

Other parts of the Act set forth standards for punishing offenders, protecting victims and students with special needs, and guides for prevention programs. Further, the Act identifies the responsibilities of central government, local governments, superintendents, and school principals. The Act also speaks about the need to have counseling teachers in schools as well as the creation of task forces and related organizations outside of schools.

Despite its various amendments, criticisms of the Act continue. First, the Act's vague and abstract definitions of school violence have created confusion leading to legal irregularities and imbalances (Jeon & Jung, 2013; Kwon, 2013). Second, the overlapping processes of superintendents, committees on school violence, principals, counseling teachers, and teachers not only causing inefficiency but also physical and mental fatigue on the part of victims (Kwon, 2013). Third, the Act does not present fundamental solutions because it focuses largely on punishing offenders rather than protecting victims (Jeon & Jung, 2013; Moon & Kang, 2015). Put another way, the Act is geared toward countermeasures after incidents occur rather than preventing the school violence.

A body of research suggests improvements for the Act. First, the Act should create a thorough systematic consultation-treatment support system that embodies a focus on prevention to minimize damages and enhance rapid recovery of the victims. Moreover, the government should resolve disputes by extending the same legal guarantees to victims of school violence as it does to crime victims. In addition, the government needs to understand and distinguish the differences in the level of damages between elementary, middle, and high school violence in order to apply the appropriate and effective measures (Jeon & Jung, 2013). Moreover, in light of reports of teachers being harmed by students, the concept of school violence should be expanded by including prohibitions of additional forms of violence (Moon & Kang, 2015).

Character Education

On December 29, 2014, Congress passed the Character Education Improvement Law; it went into effect on July 21, 2015. This law, requiring compulsory character education, is the first of its kind in the world. The purpose of the law is to develop individuals with sound and proper attitudes as citizens. According to the act's definition, "education that nurtures sound attitudes and enhances individuals' capability and personality/character that is necessary to live in harmony with other people, community, and nature." The act includes core values and virtues of character education such as: proprieties, filial duty, honesty, responsibility, respect, solicitude, communication.

This law states that the central government, local governments, and school officials are responsible for character education. In response, the government formed a committee on the Character Education Improvement Law to establish comprehensive plans every five years. Along with the comprehensive plans, local government heads and superintendents in seventeen regions will set and implement individual general plans. At the beginning of each year, school officials must report their plans for character education to superintendents and provide curriculum-based instruction on character education. Further, teachers are required to receive compulsory trainings while teacher preparation institutions must create courses designed to enhance instruction on character education.

Critics have voiced concerns about character education. First, critics point out that the controversy involves abstract concepts and has vague measurements of success (Choi, 2015; Huh, 2015; Kim, 2015; Park, 2015; Shin, 2015). Although the law contains a definition of character education, it is unclear how character education is defined, which components should be included or excluded in curricula, and how programs should be evaluated. For example, among eight values that the law suggested, proprieties and filial duty are from Confucianism while some scholars challenge these as outdated from a modern perspective (Choi, 2015; Huh, 2015; Kim, 2015). In addition, critics observed that the suggested values can be interpreted differently by individual people, leading to further confusion.

Another concern focuses on distorting the original purpose and meaning of character education (Choi, 2015; Huh, 2015; Kim, 2016). According to the law, students are to be evaluated once a year based on character education curricula. However, there are still problems in current the evaluation system which can impact student rankings and their ability to succeed on the college entrance examination. Also, the difficulties associated with the evaluation of character education may create the problem of shadow education which would result in "cram schools" or private tutoring to help students succeed (Huh, 2015; Kim, 2016).

One solution suggested by critics is to include character education in the basic curriculum, not as a separate subject but injected throughout the whole curriculum. Other suggestions call for are diversification of discussions rather than hierarchical orders, the expansion of the Character Education Promotion Committee with experienced school professionals, and the reselection of core values based on national sensitivity and modern virtues (Choi, 2015; Kim, 2015; Kim, 2016; Park, 2015).

Nuri Curriculum

Korea has two types of preschool institutions: kindergartens and the daycare centers. The terms and operations of these two institutions are different from in the United States. Both kindergartens and daycare centers serve preschool children. The difference of terminology comes from who is responsible for the institutions. The Ministry of Education is accountable for kindergarten while the Ministry of Health and Welfare oversees daycare centers.

Insofar as kindergartens and the daycare centers have different curricula, the Nuri Curriculum is the government's attempt to bring both standardized curricula for all preschool children and support for them all with free education (Jang, 2012; Jeon, 2014). The Nuri Curriculum includes physical well-being and health, communications, social relationships, art and experiences, and nature study (Ministry of Education, 2011).

When the government adopted the Nuri curriculum on May 2, 2012, it was only for five-year-old children. In 2013, the government lowered the age limit to three-year-olds, while also expanding governmental support for free education from nine years, as reflected in elementary and middle schools, to twelve years. The Nuri Curriculum aims to enhance national responsibility over early childhood education, form a social consensus, promote an increase in the birthrate, and provide equal opportunities and quality of education for all children by having this standardized curriculum (Jang, 2012).

A major concern associated with the Nuri curriculum is its budget (Jeon, 2014; Lee, Lee, & Jo, 2015) which has led to constant conflict between the central and local governments. Before the adoption of the Nuri Curriculum, financial support came from two offices, the Ministry of Education and Ministry of Health and Welfare. Presently, the budget for the Nuri Curriculum comes from Ministry of Education, a part of the central government, while financial grant local education budgets come from the local governments (Jang, Hwang, & Kim, 2012).

The persistent financial problem is how to allocate financial grants for local education budgets. On one hand, the central government claims that it is the responsibility of local government to allocate the budget. On the other hand, local governments respond that the central government has not increased the amount of financial grant it provides and so is asking local governments to allocate within the same amount of budget. In an attempt to resolve this dilemma, scholars suggest that the two levels of government should discuss a long-term developmental plan by conducting in-depth discussions about the timelines, estimate budgets thoroughly based on available resources, and standardize the usage of grants for all local governments (Kang, Hwang, & Kim, 2012; Jeon, 2014; Lee, Lee, & Jo, 2015).

CONCLUSION

Korean education has experienced exponential growth since gaining National independence in 1945. When the thirty-five years of Japanese colonial rule ended in 1945, "less than 5 percent of the adult population [combined South and North] had more than an elementary school education" (Seth, 2002: 2). Despite the odds against it, South Korean elementary education attendance reached near 100 percent in late 1950s and near 100 percent middle-school attendance in 1990s (Choi 2007). Behind this extraordinary enrollment growth were governmental policies linking educational development to economic growth, producing a qualified labor force needed for the nation's industrialization, and a series of education reforms enacted to achieve this goal.

In spite of this spectacular quantitative and qualitative growth, South Korean education also faces many challenges. In order to address growing school violence, the Act on the Prevention and Countermeasures against Violence was enacted in 2004. The public has voiced concerns about this Act, expressing a desire for its focus to be on prevention of school violence rather than on taking counter measures after incidents occur.

The Character Education Improvement Law, enacted in 2015, aims to instill civic attitudes in youths. This law is also controversial because the term itself is abstract and so raises practical concerns of how to teach as well as how to evaluate character education. Further, as to preschool education, South Koreans in general agree that it should be extended to young children. In response to public concern, then, the government enacted the Nuri Curriculum in 2012 and amended it in 2013. Still, conflict continues between central and local governments with regard to funding responsibility for this initiative.

The Korean educational system experienced transformation at the level of light speed both quantitatively and qualitatively. At the same time, Korean society rapidly transformed from one that was rural and agrarian to one of the most heavily industrialized and technologically advanced nations in the world. Moreover, challenges have arisen about the relevance of the ability of the educational system to serve national needs as Korea went through various stages of development and demographic changes. It is reasonable to expect that these social transformations have imposed tremendous challenges and pressures on the educational system. Thus, the Korean educational system is at a critical juncture as it seeks to develop schools perceived as equitable as they strive to meet the need of all stakeholders.

REFERENCES

Cheonbook Ilbo (2015, August 27). "Severe penalty recommended for a teacher who expressed and insisted his religious perspectives."

Choi, J. (2015). *Law and humanity education issues of "Character Education Promotion Act."* 21st Korea Law and Human Right Education Association Conference Book, 89–114.

Choi, S. (2007). "Schooling in South Korea." In Postiglione, G. & J. Tan (eds.). *Going to School in East Asia: The Global School Room*. Westport, CT: Greenwood. Pp. 320–343.

Clark, N. & Park, H. (2013, June 1). "Education in South Korea." *World Education and News & Reviews*. Accessed on June 8, 2016 from http://wenr.wes.org/2013/06/wenr-june-2013-an-overview-of-education-in-south-korea/.

Huh, J. (2015). "An analysis on newspaper evaluations of 'Character Education Promotion Act.'" *Law and Human Right Research, 8*(3): 175–99.

Jang, M. (2012). "Meaning of inducement and suggestions for Nuri curriculum." *Korean Education Association Conference, 2012*: 89–91.

Jang, M., Hwang, S., & Kim, M. (2012). 2013–2017 *Early childhood mid/long-term development direction*. Research report, Seoul: Korea Institute of Child Care and Education (KICCE).

Jeon, J. & Jung, S. (2013). "A study on improvements of the 'Act on the Prevention and Countermeasures against Violence in Schools': Focused on education, prevention and recovery function." *Educational Law Research, 25*(1): 205–29.

Jeon, S. (2014). "Educational policy and communication through "Nuri" Course: On the focus of newspapers." *Educational Politics Research, 21*(2): 99–126.

Kim, G. (2015). "Culture: Problems and suggestions of 'Character Education Improvement Law.'" *Korean Thought and Culture, 78*: 459–86.

Kim, N. (2016). "A critical consideration on the idea and implication of the 'Character Education Promotion Law.'" *Studies on Life and Culture, 39*: 55–102.

Kwon, O. (2013). "A study on the act of the prevention and measure to the school violence." *Contention of Law, 43*: 79–102.

Lee, J. et al. (2009). *The sixty years of Korean education*. Korea Institute of Curriculum and Instruction.

Lee, Y., Lee, K., & Jo, A. (2015). "Status and improvement of Nuri policy as free early childhood care & education." *Child Policy Research, 9*(2): 113–36.

Ministry of Education. (2011). "Nuri curriculum: Preschool curriculum amendment." *Ministry of Education*, 2011–30.

Moon, Y. & Kang, D. (2015). "A critical review about the application scope and victim protection system of the 'Act on the Prevention of and Countermeasures against Violence in Schools.'" *Law & Policy Review, 21*(1): 151–80.

OECD (2010). *Education at a Glance*. Paris: Organization for Economic Cooperation and Development.

Park, H. (2015). "Discussions with the issue of character education promotion." *Educational Law Research, 27*(3): 77–100.

Seth, M. (2002). *Education Fever: Society, Politics, and the Pursuit of Schooling in South Korea*. Center for Korean Studies, University of Hawaii Press.

Shin, Y. (2015). "A constitutional study on the concept of character and character education." *Educational Law Research, 27*(3): 101–23.

The Office of Legislation. (2016). *The Act on the Prevention and Countermeasures against Violence in Schools*. Derived from: http://www.law.go.kr/lsInfoP.do?lsiSeq=162100&efYd=20141119#0000.

DECREES AND LEGISLATION

Constitution of South Korea (1948), available at http://www.servat.unibe.ch/icl/ks00000_.html.

Decree on the Appointment of Public Education Officials, 2012. The Presidential Decree No. 23644, February 29, 2012.
Enforcement Decree of the Elementary and Secondary Education Act, 2013. Act. No. 24423, Partial Amendment, March 23, 2013.
Elementary and Secondary Education Act, 2012. Act. No. 11384, Partial Amendment, March 21, 2012.
Framework Act on Education, 2008. Act. No. 8915, Partial Amendment, March 21, 2008.
Private School Act, 2012. Act. No. 11216, Partial Amendment, January 26, 2012.
Public Education Officials Act, 2016. Act. No. 13819, Partial Amendment, January 27, 2016.

Chapter Five

Turkey

Ricardo Lozano and Irem Comoğlu

INTRODUCTION

Turkey is a land of contrasts. It is the place where east meets west, where Europe meets Asia, and where cultures and societies have competed for a privileged geographical location for centuries. In addition to having been gifted with location, Turkey's unique history has resulted in a unique multiculturalism with an abundance of culture, history, art, and a complex, sophisticated society.

Education, as any other sector in the country, is challenged by "East meets West" and finding its sense of national identity. The founding of the Turkish Republic in 1923 brought a series of changes resulting in the strengthening of the fabric of its national identity. The development of the new republic was accomplished through, among other adjustments, the introduction of basic fundamental changes in education, such as a modified Latin alphabet for the phonetic requirements of the spoken language.

NATIONAL BACKGROUND INFORMATION

Location

Turkey is located in both southeastern Europe and southwestern Asia, bordering the Black Sea, between Bulgaria and Georgia, and bordering the Aegean Sea and the Mediterranean Sea, between Greece and Syria. The country is strategically located, with 97 percent of its total land area of 814,578 km^2 in Asia and 3 percent in Europe. Additionally, Turkey controls the Bosporus, Sea of Marmara, and Dardanelles straits that link the Black and Aegean Seas (Yenen, 2011).

Brief History of Major Events

Modern Turkey was founded in 1923 from the Anatolian remnants of the defeated Ottoman Empire by Mustafa Kemal (1881–1938), later honored with the title Atatürk or "Father of the Turks." With the foundation of the Republic in 1923, a considerable reform movement started in many fields, including education, which began to Westernize many of the nation's practices. Under Atatürk's leadership, the country adopted wide-ranging social, legal, and political reforms to achieve social change and modernization, moving from an Islamic entity to a modern secular state.

The transition to the multiparty system in 1950 and military coups in 1960 and 1980 denoted important turning points in the country's history. Turkey joined the United Nations in 1945 and in 1952 it became a member of NATO. In 1964, Turkey became an associate member of the European Community. Over the past decade, the country has undertaken numerous reforms to strengthen its democracy and economy; Turkey began accession membership talks with the European Union in 2005 (CIA, 2014).

Population

Turkey has a population of 81,619,322 (2014 estimates), with a median age of 28.5. The country's age structure is as follows: 0–14 years: 25.5 percent; 15–24 years: 16.8 percent; 25–54 years: 42.9 percent; 55–64 years: 6.7 percent; 65 years and over: 8.1 percent (CIA, 2014). Life expectancy at birth in Turkey is 73.29 years, and the total fertility rate is 2.08 children born per woman. The most highly represented ethnic groups in the country are Turkish, 70 percent; Kurdish, 18 percent; and other minorities, 12 percent. (2008 estimates; CIA 2014). Turkey is 99.8 percent Muslim, with the remaining 0.2 percent mostly Christian and Jewish. Turkish is the official language, with other minority languages spoken, particularly in the East (CIA, 2014).

AN OVERVIEW OF TURKEY'S EDUCATION SYSTEM

Major Historical Events

The first modern advancements in education in Turkey appeared between 1776 and 1839 during the years of the Ottoman Empire. These involved educational reforms beginning with the establishment of military schools, the introduction of Western languages, mainly French and English, and the introduction of compulsory elementary education. Between 1878 and 1908, innovations in education took place, most notably the opening of educational institutions for individuals with physical disabilities.

Additionally during this period, the first publication of national educational statistics took place between 1894 and 1895, and books on education and training were first published in 1898. The Ministry of General Education of the Ottoman Empire was established on March 17, 1857. The Ministry has operated under the name of Ministry of National Education since 1992.

Following the establishment of the Republic in 1923, educational reforms were started in the areas of education: unification, organization, modifications in quality, and expansion. The process of social change through education propagated a deeper awareness and understanding of citizenship, as well as the development of a new and modern society (MONE 2005). Further, during the 1920s, the Caliphate, Shar'ia, and traditional medrese school systems were abolished, and the use of religion for political purposes was banned.

Education became the focus of the new state and a new education system characterized by national concern, scientific reasoning, modernization, and secularism was created. "The Law on Unification of Education" in 1924 ensured unification of education by placing all schools under the direction of the Ministry of Education (Akinoğlu, 2008; Gurşimsek, Kaptan, & Erkan, 1997).

After 1921, Commissions of Wise Men were created with the purpose of increasing the quality of education and training. Between 1939 and 1999, sixteen meetings of the Councils of National Education were also assembled with the purpose of bettering education in Turkey. These Councils continue to be the most important consultative agencies to the Ministry of Education. In order to facilitate education and increase literacy, Turkish was established as the official language and adopted the existing Latin-based alphabet in 1928. Turkey has enacted significant improvements in education since its beginnings as a republic. From 1923 to 2005, the number of schools in the country rose from 5,134 to 67,181, the number of pupils increased from 364,428 to 19,564,552, and the number of teachers increased from 12,573 to 713,390 (MONE, 2005).

Turkish Education System at a Glance

The Turkish National Education System, established by the National Education Basic Act of 1739, consists of both formal and nonformal education. Formal education refers to regular education conducted within a school for individuals in a certain age group at the same academic level. Formal education encompasses pre-primary, primary, secondary, and higher education institutions. Nonformal education serves individuals who are not part of the formal education system (MONE, 2011).

Education in Turkey is overseen by two main bodies: Yükseköğretim Kurulu (YOK, Higher Education Council), which is responsible for the planning, coordinating, and supervising of higher education, and Milli Eğitim Bakanlığı (MEB, Ministry of National Education). Public and private education institutions, both formal and nonformal, are under the supervision of the Ministry of National Education.

Turkey spends 6.5 percent of its GDP in education. Turkey's literacy rate is estimated to be 95.3 percent (98.5 males and 92.1 females). The gross enrollment ratio of female pupils in primary education is 108.8 percent, secondary—100.5 percent, and tertiary—73.2 percent (CIA, 2016; Turkish Statistical Institute, 2016; UNICEF, 2016; WDR, 2016).

LEGAL/CONSTITUTIONAL SOURCES OF EDUCATION IN TURKEY

An Overview of Turkey's Legal System

Turkey is a republic founded on the principle of the division of powers into legislative, executive and judiciary branches. The primary sources of Turkish law are the constitution, laws, law-amending ordinances, international treaties, regulations, and by-laws (Yazici, 2011); nonetheless, the Constitution is the highest body in the Turkish legal system. According to Article 11 of the Constitution:

> The provisions of the Constitution are fundamental legal rules binding upon legislative, executive and judicial organs, and administrative authorities and other institutions and individuals. Laws shall not be in conflict with the Constitution.
>
> Article 2 of the Constitution enumerates the democratic and secular features of the Republic.
>
> The Republic of Turkey is a democratic, secular and social state governed by the rule of law, bearing in mind the concepts of public peace, national solidarity and justice respecting human rights, loyal to the Atatürk nationalism and based on the fundamental tenets set forth in the Preamble.

The president, as the head of state, is elected for a five-year term. The president heads the National Security Council and represents the office of the commander in chief. Executive power is in the hands of the president and the Council of Ministers, which is headed by the prime minister. The prime minister is appointed by the president from among the members of the Turkish Grand National Assembly.

In Turkey, the prime minister nominates ministers whose appointments are subject to the approval of the Turkish Grand National Assembly. The Council of Ministers issues regulations on the application of laws and other matters, provided that they do not conflict with existing laws, and are examined by the Council of State.

Legislative power rests on the Turkish Grand National Assembly, a 550-seat, unicameral body elected under a system of proportional representation by universal adult suffrage for a five-year term. Only parties which have gathered more than 10 percent of the national vote are represented in the Assembly. The Turkish Grand National Assembly enacts, amends, and revokes laws; supervises the work of the Council of Ministers; and authorizes the Council of Ministers to issue decrees on specific matters regarding the rule of law.

The Judiciary reviews the constitutionality of laws, decrees, and the rules of procedure of the Turkish Grand National Assembly. Judicial decisions are published immediately in the official gazette and are binding for all, including the Legislative and Executive powers. Turkey has a unified legal system of civil and military courts, each with a Court of Appeals in Ankara.

An Overview of Regulations Regarding Education

The right to education in Turkey has been secured for all by Article 42 of the Constitution, establishing that "no one shall be deprived of the right of learning and education." Turkish education is organized on the basis of the Law of the Organization and Duties of the Ministry of National Education, the Basic Law of National Education, and the laws regulating the education system, as well as development plans, government programs, decision of national education councils, and regulations regarding the principles related to the types, levels, and functions of education (OECD, 2005).

The Basic Law of National Education No. 1739 establishes the aims of the Turkish National Education System:

> To raise all individuals as citizens who are committed to the principles and reforms of Atatürk and to the nationalism of Atatürk as expressed in the Constitution, who adopt, protect and promote the national, moral, human, spiritual and cultural values of the Turkish Nation, who love and always seek to exalt their family, country and nation, who know their duties and responsibilities towards the Republic of Turkey which is a democratic, secular and social state governed by the rule of law, founded on human rights and on the tenets laid down in the preamble to the Constitution, and who have internalized these in their behavior;
>
> To raise them as constructive, creative and productive persons who are physically, mentally, morally, spiritually and emotionally balanced, have a sound personality and character, with the ability to think freely and scientifically and have a broad worldview, that are respectful for human rights, value personality and enterprise, and feel responsibility towards society;
>
> To prepare them for life by developing their interests, talents and capabilities and providing them with the necessary knowledge, skills and attitudes and the habit of working with others and to ensure that they acquire a profession which shall make them happy and contribute to the happiness of society.

INSTITUTIONAL ISSUES

Compulsory Attendance

One of the most important recent reforms in the Turkish education system has been the transition from a five-year compulsory education system to eight years of compulsory education. Law no. 4306, dated August 18, 1997, extended compulsory primary education to eight years. More recently, with the adoption of Primary Education Law no. 6287 on March 30, 2012, a radical decision was made in the Turkish education system when compulsory education increased from eight to twelve years beginning in the 2012–2013 academic year. In this new system, known as "4 + 4 + 4," compulsory education was reorganized into three levels: 4 years of primary education, 4 years lower-secondary, and 4 years of upper-secondary education.

This new law, enacted as "Law on Making Amendments on Primary Education Law," brought about significant changes in the national primary education system. The law requires educational authorities to provide education in separate buildings for children attending primary, lower-secondary, and upper-secondary schools. The law also mandates the inclusion of elective courses in lower-secondary schools to be prepared and offered according to students' abilities, development, and preferences. Further, the law establishes the provision of *Imam Hatip* lower-secondary schools, vocational schools to train government-employed imams, and courses such as "the Quran" and "the Life of the Prophet Mohammed" to be offered as elective courses in lower and upper-secondary schools.

Funding for Public Education

Insofar as Turkey has a highly centralized governance structure, and the country's education policy is regulated by the Ministry of National Education (MONE), local school officials typically have little autonomy and are often unable to respond to their local needs. Education is publicly funded, but schools can also receive contributions from parents through their local school-parent associations. Even though overall school funding has increased in Turkey in recent years, primary and secondary education are underfunded when compared to other OECD countries (OECD, 2013).

In recent years, the Turkish government has increased education funding toward *Imam Hatip* schools, and religious education in public schools. This decision provoked intense controversies with regard to the proper role of Islam in public life.

Conversely, a significant number of families in more affluent, progressive, and liberal regions of the country choose private education for their children. Although significantly more expensive than public education, private education in Turkey provides smaller size classes, well qualified teachers, a range of extracurricular activities, and access to study foreign, mainly European, languages. As of the 2014–2015 academic year, the Ministry of National Education provides funding for students attending private schools. According to the Decree for the Provision of Educational Support to Students Attending Private Schools during the 2015–2016 School Year, published in the Official Gazette on July 3, 2015, the Ministry has provided private education funding for a total of 230,000 students (MONE, 2015b).

Programs of Study

Lower-secondary schools in Turkey allow choice among different elective courses such as foreign languages, environment and science, drama, and intelligence games within school campuses. Additionally, lower-secondary age students may choose religious courses in separate *Imam Hatip* religious schools. Upper-secondary education includes general, vocational, and technical education institutions with at least four years of compulsory formal or non-formal education.

The Ministry of National Education establishes the aims and duties of secondary education in Turkey:

1. To enable all students to have the awareness and power to get to know the problems provided that giving culture on minimum common general level look for ways of solution and acquire [sic] the consciousness of contributing to country's economic, social and cultural development and power.
2. To prepare students for higher education or for life and job fields in accordance with their interests, aptitude and abilities with various programs and schools. While these missions are accomplished, a balance is set between students' expectations and abilities and the needs of the society (MONE, 2015a, p. xiii).

Secondary education in the country is classified in three main categories:

General Secondary Education

This is a four-year compulsory educational process designed to prepare students both for higher education and for the future according to their interests, expectations, and abilities. This also equips students with world knowledge with an education-based on primary education.

Vocational and Technical Secondary Education

This is a four-year compulsory educational process to prepare students both for higher education. This also readies students for the future as well as for occupations and job fields according to their interests, expectations, and abilities in addition to equipping them with world knowledge with an education based on primary education.

Open Upper-Secondary High School

This offers education to students who are unable to attend formal educational institutions providing face-to-face education, who have completed the formal education stage in terms of age, and who wish to follow an open upper-secondary high school while attending upper-secondary high school. In this system, education is provided on a pass or fail and a credit system; there are no classes and teachers because the system does not require them (MONE, 2015a, p. xiii, xiv). Both public and private schools in Turkey are governed by the Ministry of National Education.

FACULTY RIGHTS

Due Process Rights in Hiring, Promotion and Tenure, and Dismissal

Teacher assignment and transfer policies are handled according to Regulation no. 293229 for Teacher Assignment and Transfer, published in the Official Gazette on April 17, 2015. Teacher employment policies including assignment and transfer are regulated centrally by the Ministry of National Education. Teachers are allocated to schools through the Ministry's initial assignments of novice teachers or seniority-based transfers. Teachers who have worked in less developed regions of the country receive an annual higher seniority score compared to their counterparts working in more developed regions (Ozoglu, 2015).

Another important factor affecting teacher assignment is the Civil Servant Selection Examination, known as KPSS in Turkish. The KPSS, administered by the Student Selection and Placement Center (ÖSYM), consists of multiple-choice questions on general knowledge along with ability, general culture, and educational sciences. Teachers are assigned to public schools throughout the country according to their KPSS scores. For teachers choosing to work in the private sector, KPSS scores are not mandatory. The complexity of the KPSS system, the lack of questions directly related to their subject area, the fear of not being appointed to their preferred locations, and the thought of being considered unsuccessful if one fails the KPSS have been identified as significant sources of stress for many Turkish student teachers (Can, 2010).

In order to motivate teachers wanting to further their professional careers, the Teaching Profession Career Ladder Program (TPCLP) was put into practice in line with Regulation no 25905 on Teaching Career Ladder Advancement, published in the Official Gazette on August 13, 2005. The TPCLP consists of four levels: teacher candidate, teacher, expert teacher, and lead teacher.

The first step concerns beginning teachers who are in a period of candidacy for one or two years. Teachers who have been working for more than seven years may apply for the "expert teacher" level. According to this program, teachers' advancement in their careers is based on their seniority, examination results for TPCLP, and their participation in various professional development activities. The program especially values participation in professional development activities which are considered to be important for the development of teachers' professional skills, motivation, and education quality (Ozdemir, 2013).

Freedom of Speech

Articles 24, 25, 26, and 27 of the Constitution of 1982 state the provision of freedoms with regards to religion, thought, expression, and research:

> Article 24
>
> Everyone has the right to freedom of conscience, religious belief and conviction.
>
> Article 25
>
> Everyone has the right to freedom of thought and opinion. No one shall be compelled to reveal his thoughts and opinions for any reason or purpose, nor shall anyone be blamed or accused on account of his thoughts and opinions.
>
> Article 26 (as amended on October 17, 2001)
>
> Everyone has the right to express and disseminate his thoughts and opinions by speech, in writing, or in pictures or through other media, individually or collectively. This right includes the freedom to receive and impart information and ideas without interference from official authorities. This provision shall not preclude subjecting transmission by radio, television, cinema, and similar means to a system of licensing.
>
> (Amended as of October 3, 2001, Act No. 4709). The exercise of these freedoms may be restricted for the purposes of protecting national security, public order and public safety, the basic characteristics of the Republic, and safeguarding the indivisible integrity of the State with its territory and nation, preventing crime, punishing offenders, withholding information duly classified as a state secret, protecting the reputation and rights, and private and

family life of others, or protecting professional secrets as prescribed by law, or ensuring the proper functioning of the judiciary.

(Added as of October 3, 2001, Act No. 4709). The formalities, conditions and procedures to be applied in exercising the right to expression and dissemination of thought shall be prescribed by law.

Article 27

Everyone has the right to study and teach freely, explain, and disseminate science and arts and to carry out research in these fields.

The right to disseminate shall not be exercised for the purpose of changing the provisions of articles 1, 2, and 3 of the Constitution.

The provision of this article shall not preclude regulation by law of the entry and distribution of foreign publications in the country.

Freedom of Association/Unions

The Turkish Constitution does not prevent civil servants, including teachers and school administrators, from becoming members of unions:

ARTICLE 51 (as amended on October 3, 2001; Act No. 4709)

Employees and employers have the right to form unions and higher organizations, without prior permission, and they also possess the right to become a member of a union and to freely withdraw from membership, in order to safeguard and develop their economic and social rights and the interests of their members in their labor relations. No one shall be forced to become a member of a union or to withdraw from membership.

The right to form a union shall be solely restricted by law on the grounds of national security, public order, prevention of commission of crime, public health, public morals and protecting the rights and freedoms of others.

The formalities, conditions and procedures to be applied in exercising the right to form union shall be prescribed by law.

(Repealed on September 12, 2010; Act No.5982)

The scope, exceptions and limits of the rights of civil servants who do not have a worker status are prescribed by law in line with the characteristics of their services.

The regulations, administration and functioning of unions and their higher bodies shall not be inconsistent with the fundamental characteristics of the Republic and principles of democracy.

Similarly, no article in Law no. 657 on Civil Servants prevents civil servants from establishing unions and becoming members of unions. Law no. 4688 on Civil Servant Unions, dated June 25, 2001, establishes the rules for forming or joining unions or confederations. Considering the number of education unions in Turkey, the majority of education union members in the country (98 percent) belong to one of the four education unions, namely, *Türk Eğitim Sen, Eğitim Sen, Eğitim Bir Sen, and Eğitim İş* (Kayikci, 2013).

Insofar as instruction on legal foundations of education is virtually nonexistent in teacher education programs in Turkey, most teachers are completely unaware of their legal rights. Teachers in Turkey also consider union membership to be a political act because being a member of a union is considered to adhere fully to the ideology represented by the particular union. Because unions in Turkey are considered political bodies, it is difficult to perceive that their duties and responsibilities toward their members are unambiguously fulfilled.

STUDENT RIGHTS

The Admissions Process

According to Regulation 29072 for Pre-school and Primary Education Institutions published in the Official Gazette on July 26, 2013, student registration for state schools is completed online through the national electronic school system. School registration and placement is based on students' address consistent with the national address database. Students of foreign origin who are not Turkish citizens, but have identity numbers, are admitted to schools according to the information in their residence permit or passport. Legislation on preschool and primary education does not make reference to issues of race, gender, disability, and/or religion as part of the admission process.

Regulation 28758 for Secondary Education Institutions published in the Official Gazette on September 7, 2013, establishes that students completing lower-secondary school are admitted to upper-secondary schools according to their Transition from Primary to Secondary Education (TEOG) examination scores, and/or their ability test scores, based on personal preferences. Based on their preferences, students are placed in schools admitting pupils within their TEOG score range, their ability levels, and their interview and/or physical capacity results. Students older than eighteen years of age or married are not admitted to secondary schools.

The Provincial Directorate of National Education is responsible for the admissions process of students in need of alternative educational services. The Commission of Student Placement and Transfer within the Provincial Directorate of National Education is responsible for the admission and transfer processes of students of foreign nationality. Students of foreign nationality are required to have student visas. Students with unknown nationalities, or who are refugees, are not required to have student visas.

Student Discipline

Generally

Pursuant to Regulation 28758 for Secondary Education Institutions, objection to disciplinary penalties is conducted by the school manager, the student, if older than eighteen years of age or the students' parents. The process must be conducted within five days following the notification for disciplinary action. School managers are responsible for sending the objections to disciplinary actions to the Discipline Board within five working days.

Lower-Secondary School Students

The disciplinary actions to be taken toward lower-secondary students resulting from their involvement in reprehensible actions are stated in Regulation 29072 for Pre-school and Primary Education Institutions published in the Official Gazette on July 26, 2013.

Verbal Warnings

These sanctions are used when, for example, students come to school late; are continually absent without excuses; extend periods of permission given by school officials without excuses; display bad manners; lie; fail to keep the walls, desks, and school clean; and/or keeping their mobile phone on during lessons.

Written Censures

These punishments are applied when, for instance, students exhibit arrogant or disrespectful behavior toward administrators, teachers, other school staff, or peers; they ignore school rules and disrupt the learning environment; interrupt school sponsored activities; continual lying, cheating; falsifying official records; disobeying the dress code; smoking; and/or fighting.

Expulsions from School

This most serious form of punishment is imposed, by way of illustration, on students who violate the fundamental principles of the Constitution; commit sexual assaults; insult, slander, and or threaten others in school; carry weapons within school premises; misuse school materials; commit acts of discrimination; damage the belongings of others; attack administrators or teachers; and/or promote the use of alcohol or other habit-forming substances.

Upper-Secondary School Students

The disciplinary actions to be taken toward upper-secondary school students as the result of their involvement in specific reprehensible actions are stated in Regulation 28758 for Secondary Education Institutions published in the Official Gazette on September 7, 2013.

Written Censures

These are applied when, for example, students fail to keep the school and school materials clean and tidy; fail to fulfill duties required by teachers or administrators; violate the established dress code; smoke; handle the belongings of others without their consent; lie; and/or are absent without excuses.

Short-Term Suspensions

These are used when, for instance, students engage in sexual and verbal harassment; insult, slander, or discriminate against others; insult teachers, administrators, or other staff; are caught fighting, bullying, and/or gambling.

Expulsions from School

This form of punishment is imposed, by way of illustration, when students, by way of illustration, act with disrespect toward the Turkish flag or any other national or state symbols; denigrating national and spiritual values; insulting these values; theft; damaging of school property; disrupting classes, exams or other activities; use or possession of habit-forming substances; and/or coercing others to engage in illicit activities.

Expulsions from Formal Education

This most serious form of punishment is applied for such acts of misbehavior as insulting the Turkish flag or any other national or state symbols; taking individual or collective action against the fundamental principles of the Constitution; organizing or being involved in divisive actions with the purpose of discriminating against individuals on the basis of language, ethnicity, sex or political, philosophical, and/or religious beliefs; disrupting the actions of school committees; trading habit-forming substances; disrupting the learning environment; forming gangs; kidnapping; and/or theft for ransom.

Despite the rigorous disciplinary legal system existing in Turkey, the prevalent social consciousness favors the notion that adults possess the right to punish misbehaving children and that teachers have the right to children if they "deserve it" (Turkum 2010). Thus, corporal punishment is prevalent within both family and school ambits. Accordingly, a significant percentage of children in Turkey are subjected to different forms of corporal punishment in schools. Additionally, there are teachers who believe in the necessity of physical punishment for the development of children (Gozutok, Er, & Karacaoglu, 2006).

At the same time, the Ministry of National Education issued circulars 1995, 2003, 2005, and 2006 designed to help prevent violence in schools. In accordance with the 2006 circular, a commission should be established in every school with the purpose of developing action plans for the prevention of violence (Turkum, 2010). However, in reality, physical and verbal abuses are prevalent in Turkish schools. In practice, corporal punishment is tolerated, unpunished, and mostly overlooked not only by school teachers and administrators, but also by society as a whole (Lozano & Kizilaslan, 2013).

Search and Seizure/ Drug Testing

As indicated in Regulation 28758 for Secondary Education Institutions, when needed for student safety, members of the School Reward and Punishment Board, and commissioned teachers may search buildings, desks, and other places to prevent improper student behavior from turning into crimes, to provide security of educational environments, and to protect students against improper and harmful behavior. Regulations in Turkey do not make reference to student drug testing.

Freedom of Religion

Both Regulation 29072 for Pre-school and Primary Education Institutions along with Regulation 28758 for Secondary Education Institutions allow for the establishment of suitable places for prayer, if requested.

Student dress codes at Ministry of National Education schools are determined by Regulation 28480, dated November 27, 2012. Students in primary and secondary schools are not required to wear uniforms. Pupils are required to be clean and tidy in their appearance. Girls may wear headscarves at *Imam Hatip* secondary schools in all courses. Girls in primary and secondary schools may wear headscarves in the elective course "the Quran." Even so, students are not allowed to:

- Display badges or symbols apart from their school badges,
- Wear clothes harmful to their health and/or that is improper for the season,
- Wear torn/perforated and/or transparent clothes,
- Wear shorts, tights, mini-skirts, slit skirts, short pants, sleeveless shirts, and/or t-shirts,
- Use scarves, hats, bags, and/or other accessories displaying political symbols, and/or
- Wear makeup, have dyed hair, and/or growing mustaches or beards.

Students with Special Needs

Turkey provides education to a total population of 16,379,852 students between early childhood and secondary education in general schools, including students in vocational education programs. These students are educated by a total of 795,519 teachers. Additionally, 1,268 specialized schools provide education for 288,489 pupils with special needs. These children are educated by 11,595 teachers in these specialized schools (MONE, 2016).

The history of special education in Turkey dates back to the years of the Ottoman Empire, when schools for gifted and talented students were established as part of the *enderun* schools in the mid-1400s. Following this innovation, education was provided for deaf and blind students by Istanbul Trade School (*Istanbul Ticaret Mektebi*) in 1889. Following the collapse of the Ottoman Empire in 1919, the provision of special education was discontinued in these schools, but was later reinstated following the founding of the Republic in 1923 (Ozsoy, Ozyurek, & Eripek,1998).

The Constitution of the Republic of Turkey, dated October 9, 1982, in its forty-second article, secures the right to education for all stating that "no one shall be deprived of the right of learning and education." Article 42 also provides the basis for the provision of special education in the country as it declares that "the State shall take necessary measures to rehabilitate those in need of special training as to render such people useful to society."

In 1983, the Turkish Special Education Needs Legislation came into practice. With this legislation, it was established that students with special needs should receive the education necessary to enable them to be integrated fully into society. The legislation was revised in 1997 when Special Education Law 573 came into existence. According to this law, the major principles of special education in Turkey are that all children in need of special education will benefit from such services, that special education will start at an early age, and that these services will be provided, as possible, through the inclusion of students with special needs into mainstream education with the assistance of individualized education plans.

EMERGING ISSUES

IMMIGRATION FROM WAR-TORN REGIONS IN THE MIDDLE EAST

Conflict in Turkey's Southeast Border

As a result of the recent multilateral military conflicts faced by Syria, Turkey has found itself in the middle of the migration crisis between the Middle East and Europe. Located between the conflict area and the potential shelter provided by Europe, Turkey has, by means of its geographical location, become a strategic player on this complex geopolitical struggle.

As of the first trimester of 2016, Turkey hosted over two and a half million Syrian refugees. Up until the beginning of 2013, Syrian refugees in Turkey lived in camps funded and managed by the Turkish state. Still, as a result of the limited capacities of the camps and the high number of refugees arriving daily, today most Syrian refugees reside in other towns and cities under rather difficult conditions without access to the most basic social and financial services (Icduygu, 2015).

It is estimated that more than half of the Syrian refugees in Turkey are children. Yet despite the efforts of multiple government, international, and civil organizations, education of refugee children remains the most important challenge faced by Turkey. Currently, only approximately 75,000 children, out of the half million in need of education, have access to schooling in refugee camps.

In refugee camps, schools provide education in Arabic while following the Syrian curriculum. Children and youth with residence permits are allowed to live outside of these camps and attend public schools. Students living illegally in the country are also allowed to attend schools. Access to education for children illegally living in the country is provided without proper official registration (Bircan & Sunata, 2015).

The Challenges

Given the constantly increasing number of immigrant children in Turkey, education for all is simply impossible to attain in the southeast provinces of the country. This situation calls for provisions and regulations mandating universal access to education in Turkey, and for the incorporation of regulations regarding refugee children and their access to educational services.

Another challenge presented by the current migration crisis is that numerous Syrian families are hesitant to send their daughters to schools, especially in a foreign land. In order to provide girls with access to education, and as a response to families' opposition to providing formal education to their daughters, the establishment of schools focusing on girls' education must be considered.

Despite the fact that schools in refugee camps provide education in Arabic, the need for immigrants to learn Turkish is a key component in the process of their assimilation and integration into Turkish culture and society. Currently, and particularly in the eastern part of the country, the need for speaking Turkish has been underestimated because large portions of the eastern Turkish population are familiar with indigenous languages of the region such as Arabic and Kurdish. Even so, in order for these new immigrants to be assimilated and integrated into mainstream Turkish society, Turkish language learning must be a priority for educators working with immigrant students.

As stated above, one of the most significant challenges of formulating immigrant integration policies is the education of Syrian refugee children. However, the Turkish public education system is based on a predominantly unilingual system that cannot readily offer language accommodations for foreign children. At the local level, municipalities seem to have overcome this issue, to a limited extent, by offering classes in Arabic and Kurdish, Turkish language classes, and vocational training courses for youth and adults. Local municipalities in East Turkey are also contributing to the building and running of "Syrian schools." Yet funding for teacher salaries for these schools remains a challenge for Turkish authorities.

An additional, and critical issue faced by Turkey as a part of the current migration crisis, is the "brain drain" of Syrian refugees to Europe. Most well-educated and affluent refugees have been able to immigrate to Europe whose immigration laws give preferential treatment to professional immigrants, while Turkey was slow to adjust its immigration policies to incentivize them to remain in the country. It is, therefore, imperative for Turkey to act promptly to implement policies to attract and retain more educated and qualified Syrian refugees. Policies must also provide avenues for qualified refugees to support their compatriots as they transition and become assimilated into their host country and culture. Again, though, such policies must integrate systematic and meticulous strategies specifically designed for cultured refugees, including programs and incentives designed for their training, recruitment, and retention.

CONCLUSION

The Turkish education system has profited from the experience accumulated through years of numerous developmental phases since before the foundation of the Republic. Accordingly, substantial experience has been gained as a result of the development of diverse models with regard to strategy and policy in education. The current legal centralization and control of the educational system, though, is the main hindrance to the advancement of education through independent and creative thinking.

In the recent past, during the years following the foundation of the Republic, Turkey made serious strides toward the modernization of its educational system. In more recent years, though, changes in regulations in education have been perceived to be a part of a plan to regress from the secular system established in the beginnings of the republic, to one promoting the intertwining of religion and education. These changes have the potential to provide for an increased number of government-sponsored, Islamic educational institutions throughout the country.

Primary School Education Law 6287 enacted in 2012, allowing distance education and apprenticeships beginning at age ten, has raised concerns among critics because it would allow for the removal of girls from schools, and for the starting of formal religious education for boys prior to the completion of their compulsory years of public education. Further, academic achievement levels have been observed to decline after the implementation of Education Law 6287 (Turkish Education Volunteers Foundation, 2014).

With regard to safety in schools in Turkey, the existence of plans for the prevention of violence has not impeded the physical and verbal abuses prevalent in schools, thereby exposing the reality that these laws and mandates are, essentially, unheeded. Teacher preparation programs in Turkey integrated classroom management as an academic discipline in 1998. Courses in classroom management are mainly theoretical in nature and inconsequential with regard to practical issues of misbehavior in schools. Moreover, instruction on legal foundations of education is virtually nonexistent in teacher education programs in the country. This has the potential for causing serious legal disputes between educators and families.

The Turkish education system would greatly benefit from the development and implementation of practical instruction in classroom management and legal foundations of education. A knowledgeable teaching force in these subjects would contribute to the modernization of the Turkish classroom.

Finally, the pressing issue of immigration resulting from Turkey's geographical location between the Middle East and Europe has left close to one million migrant children without access to basic educational services in the country. Turkey is in desperate need of mandates supporting the education of migrant children, the education of students in their native languages, as well as the introduction of Turkish language learning programs for all immigrants planning to remain in the country. Additionally, Turkey must provide avenues for the education of girls whose families are not comfortable sending them to schools in a foreign land. And, lastly, the country would profit greatly from programs geared toward the assimilation of well-educated, affluent Middle Eastern immigrants into Turkey. These highly educated Middle Eastern immigrants have the potential to function as liaisons for their less fortunate compatriots in their process of assimilation into their host country and culture.

The effect of the recently implemented educational legislation for primary and secondary education in Turkey, in addition to the effect of the current migration crisis experienced in the region, are yet to be determined. Despite its history and long-held traditions and culture, Turkey, given the blessing and curse of its geographical location, remains in search of the balance and identity hoped for throughout its history.

REFERENCES

Akinoğlu, O. (2008). "Primary education curriculum reforms in Turkey." *Online Submission*, 3(2): 195–99.

Bircan, T. and Sunata, U. (2015). "Educational assessment of Syrian refugees in Turkey." *Migration Letters*, 12(3): 226–37.

Can, S. (2010). "Organizational stressors for the student teachers in state universities." *Procedia Social and Behavioral Sciences*, 2: 4853–57.

CIA (2014). *The World Fact Book*. Available at https://www.cia.gov/library/publications/the-world-factbook/geos/ar.html.

CIA (2016). *The World Fact Book*. Available at https://www.cia.gov/library/publications/the-world-factbook/geos/au.html.

Council of Higher Education. (2017). *Higher education system in Turkey*. Available at http://www.yok.gov.tr/en/web/cohe/higher-education-system.

Gozutok, F. D., Er, K. O., and Karacaoglu, O. C. (2006). "Okulda dayak: 1992 ve 2006 yılları karşılaştırması." *Bilim ve Aklın Aydınlığında Egitim* 75: 227–35.

Gursimşek, I., Kaptan,, F. and Erkan, S. (1997). "General view of teacher education policies of Turkey." Paper presented at The American Association of Colleges for Teacher Education. Phoenix, AZ.

Icduygu, A. (2015). "Syrian refugees in Turkey: The long road ahead." Transatlantic Council on Migration. Available at http://www.migrationpolicy.org/research/syrian-refugees-turkey-long-road-ahead.

Kayikci, K. (2013). "Unionization in the public and education sector in Turkey, and expectations of school administrators and teachers from unions." *Amme İdaresi Dergisi*, 46(1): 99–126.

Lozano, R. and Kizilaslan, I. (2013). "Approaches to classroom discipline in Turkey and their implications for teacher education." *International Journal on New Trends in Education and Their Implications*, (4)1: 180–87.

MONE (2005). "Basic education in Turkey: Background report." *Reviews of National Policies for Education*. Available at https://www.oecd.org/education/school/39642601.pdf.

MONE (2011). "National education statistics: Formal education 2010/2011." Available at http://sgb.meb.gov.tr/istatistik/meb_istatistikleri_orgun_egitim_2010_2011.pdf.

MONE (2015a). "National education statistics: Formal education 2014/2015." Available at http://sgb.meb.gov.tr/istatistik/meb_istatistikleri_orgun_egitim_2014_2015.pdf.

MONE (2015b). "Press statement." Available at http://www.meb.gov.tr/press-statement/haber/9457/en.

MONE (2016). "National education statistics, formal education 2015/2016." Available at http://sgb.meb.gov.tr/meb_iys_dosyalar/2016_03/30044345_meb_istatistikleri_orgun_egitim_2015_2016.pdf

OECD (2005). "Reviews of national policies for education—basic education in Turkey." Available at http://www.oecd.org/turkey/reviewsofnationalpoliciesforeducation-basiceducationinturkey.htm.

OECD (2013). "Education policy outlook: Turkey. Available at http://www.oecd.org/edu/EDUCATION%20POLICY%20OUTLOOK%20TURKEY_EN.pdf.

Ozdemir, S. M. (2013). "Exploring Turkish teachers' professional development experiences and their needs for professional development." *Mevlana International Journal of Education (MIJE)*, 3(4), 250–64.

Ozoglu, M. (2015). "Teacher allocation policies and the unbalanced distribution of novice and senior teachers across regions in Turkey." *Australian Journal of Teacher Education*, 40(10), 16–32.

Ozsoy, Y., Ozyurek, M., and Eripek, S. (1998). "Özel egitime muhtaç çocuklar 'Özel egitime giris.'" Ankara: Karatape Yayınları.

Republic of Turkey (2017). *Ministry of national education*. Retrieved from http://www.meb.gov.tr/meb_haberindex.php?dil=en.

Turkish Education Volunteers Foundation (TEGV). (2014). Available at http://erg.sabanciuniv.edu/sites/erg.sabanciuniv.edu/files/444.ArastirmaRaporu.04.03.14.WEB__0.pdf.

Turkish Statistical Institute. (2016). Available at http://www.turkstat.gov.tr/PreHaberBultenleri.do?id=18688.

Turkum, A. S. (2010). "Stance against violence in schools: School staff's ethical roles in the wellbeing of students in Turkey." *Cultura, Internafional Journal of Philosophy of Culture and Axiology* (2010): 164–70.

UNICEF (2016). "Humanitarian Action For Children." Available at http://www.worldbank.org/content/dam/Worldbank/Publications/WDR/WDR%202016/WDR2016_overview_presentation.pdf.

World Development Report (WDR). (2016). Available at http://www.worldbank.org/content/dam/Worldbank/Publications/WDR/WDR%202016/WDR2016_overview_presentation.pdf.

Yazıcı, S. (2011). "Update: A guide to Turkish public law and legal research." Available at http://www.nyulawglobal.org/globalex/Turkey1.html.

Yenen, S. (2011). "Turkish odyssey." Available at http://www.turkishodyssey.com/.

Chapter Six

Analysis and Reflections

Charles J. Russo

INTRODUCTION

As important as education is, individuals cannot assert this right absent the existence of legal systems establishing effective school systems under the law. As such, respect for basic rights such as teaching and learning is a long-established tenet in most countries. Thus, in all five of the countries covered in this book, China, Israel, Palestine, South Korea, and Turkey, both students and teachers have an array of rights that are explicitly identified and protected in varying degrees.

The leaders in the education law systems described in this volume strive to meet the duties as assigned by their national governments or decentralized public authorities in their provinces, states and/or territories. Moreover, educational law, and its accompanying policies, is a topic of intense public concern, regardless of whether it is governed centrally at the national level or more locally at the provincial, state, or territorial level. The fundamental roles of teachers in these systems, namely providing education to the children in their classes, is thus rightly seen as a key component of their governments as they charged with the duty of public service and protecting the common good by helping to shape educated citizens.

It is important to keep in mind that national systems described throughout this volume, combined with the statutory basis embedded in a human rights culture, are indispensable for the creation of an effective teaching and learning environment. However, this appears to be only one side of the coin. On the flip side of the coin, it is equally as important to bear in mind that as important as the law is, teaching and learning takes place in classrooms, not in legislative chambers or courtrooms. Education is thus essentially a social science founded on the dynamics of sound relationships and mutual respect that must occur in environments where all share the interest of providing the holistic common good for children and society.

SUMMARY AND ANALYSIS

In order to provide a sense of what this book is all about this section briefly reviews similarities and differences in the national education law systems described in this volume.

Legal Systems

Without saying so directly, all of the legal systems the five nations described in the volume seek to apply what can broadly be described as the rule of law with well-developed or emerging series of laws addressing education. While only Israel does not have a formal written constitution, it does have a broad collection of statutes and a growing body of litigation on education law. The most noticeable exception as to statutory guidance exists in Palestine which lacks one clear education law due to the fragmented nature of legal jurisdiction and geographic divisions following years of ongoing conflict in the region. However, a comprehensive education law has been drafted and is awaiting review, and presumably adoption, by the executive body of the Palestinian Legislative Council.

There is scant reported litigation on education law in almost all of the countries reported on in this volume. In fact, with the exception of Israel, noted above, none of the education law systems in the nations discussed in this book have much case law to offer. However, change may be in the offing, at least in China, traditionally a code law country, which has witnessed an upswing in case law which is starting to play an increasingly important role in dispute resolution related to education.

Institutional Issues

Compulsory Attendance

All of the nations reviewed in this book starting no later than age six—with Israel beginning at five while South Korea has a preschool option for children at the age of three—and lasting for varying periods of time and with differing degrees of responsibility to ensure that parents send their children to school, whether public, non-public. Only China and Israel explicitly recognize homeschooling as an option; although many parents have embraced it, homeschooling remains controversial in China.

Children in China who have reached the age of six must attend schools for nine years in elementary and lower-secondary education while those in

Singapore must attend schools between the ages of six and fifteen. In Malaysia children must attend through the completion of elementary school or sixth grade. While neither kindergarten nor secondary education is compulsory in Palestine, starting at age six students must attend school through grades nine or ten depending on whether they are subject to Israeli or Jordanian law.

Two nations introduced significant changes with regard to compulsory attendance in 2012. By introducing the Nuri curriculum, making early childhood education available in the form of preschools or day care centers, South Korea expanded governmental support for free education from age nine, culminating in middle school, to twelve years. Moreover, Turkey, increased the number of years students must attend school from eight to twelve.

School Funding and Types: Public and Non-Public

Nations around the world, including those reviewed in this volume, recognize a wide variety of types of schools. Israel and South Korea provide varying levels of funding for both government and nongovernment schools, including those that are religiously affiliated. On the other hand, the governments in China and Palestine restrict funding to state schools. At the same time, all of the nations discussed in the book are home to a variety of public and non-public schools whether religious or internationally based with the latter serving children of diplomats and residential expats.

Governance

The common feature among the governance models in the five nations discussed in this book is that they are centralized. In China, matters of governance, planning, coordination, and matters of educational management are centralized under the auspices of the Ministry of Education, the nation's highest education authority. Departments of Education at the provincial level and educational bureaus at city and county levels in China oversee educational issues in their respective areas. Also, the Ministry of Education in Palestine is the primary institution in charge of educational development management though the degree of control varies depending on where individual schools are located.

South Korea's Ministry of Education is the central government office overseeing the education sector. As for local authorities, sixteen Metropolitan/Provincial Offices of Education are located in seven major cities and nine provinces overseeing local educational administration of schools within their jurisdictions. Turkey has a highly centralized governance structure with the country's education policy is regulated by the Ministry of National Education, leaving little autonomy to local school officials who are often unable to respond to their local needs. Even so, principals in individual schools have a fair degree of authority that they have increasingly shared with teachers and parents through various school councils and committees.

Safety and Liability Issues

China, although not applying common law principles, has a broadly analogous system designed to protect children from negligence. Further, China explicitly rejected in loco parentis, instead, imposing a general duty of care on school officials to safeguard and protect students. Consequently, and, unless otherwise specified in law, negligence is a necessary condition for school liability to be imposed in China. The remaining nations covered in this book certainly are vigilant as to student safety but lack principles as well established as those at common law.

In what is certainly a sign of the times, along with the fact that all of the nations have a variety of nondiscrimination laws in place to safeguard students and teachers, they are extending their laws to cover more contemporary sources of harm to children. For example, school officials in China are focusing on the use of cell phones as a means of engaging in this unacceptable behavior.

By enacting a controversial new law aimed at ending violence in schools, South Korea, too, has addressed school safety along with its goal of preventing occurrences of bullying and harassment in schools. Finally, acknowledging problems with sexual harassment in schools and other types of harassment outside of schools, lawmakers and educators in Palestine are taking steps to eliminate such mistreatment of students.

Faculty Rights

Due Process in Employment and Dismissal

In varying degrees, the education law systems in all of the nations reviewed in this volume offer protections for teachers throughout their professional careers via a combination of statutory and common law principles. Additionally, these systems address qualifications for teachers, particularly in public schools, requiring them to meet professional standards and safeguarding their rights to employment in China, South Korea, and Turkey. Most of these nations not only require teachers to register their professional status with appropriate government agencies, but also have adopted statutory due process protections for teachers who face the loss of the jobs due to poor performance or other reasons.

Freedom of Speech

The national legal systems in all of the nations reviewed in this book recognize the rights to freedom of speech and association in the form of creating and joining unions. In China, the Ministry of Education selects teaching content and curricula but does encourage teachers to speak freely as they explore and adopt appropriate instructional methods. Palestine's Amended Basic Law of 2003 guarantees freedom of opinion and self-expression while encouraging academic research by teachers. Similarly, Turkey's Constitution of 1982 recognizes the rights to freedom of religion, thought, expression, and research. Freedom of speech of teachers in South Korea is mainly related to Educational Neutrality, particularly in the political sphere, a right discussed in the Constitution and variety of other laws.

Freedom of Association/Unions

A right closely associated with speech is freedom of association. Accordingly, teachers' unions or professional associations are present in all of the nations covered in this book and often wield considerable clout in schools. For example, teacher unions in Israel were in the forefront challenging school reform initiatives. South Korean law specifies that teacher unions may not engage in political activities or industrial actions, including strikes, work slowdowns, or other activities hindering normal business operations of the schools. Although the law in China is not explicit about whether teachers have the right to strike, it imposes a duty on unions to negotiate with employers if work stoppages or slowdowns occur. It thus appears that insofar as they are civil servants, teachers in China do not have a right to strike.

Freedom of Religion

The Constitutions and/or statutes in Palestine, South Korea, and Turkey guarantee freedom of religion in varying degrees, occasionally allowing officials to limit its exercise so as to not engender violence and create disruptions in schools.

Protection from Discrimination

Insofar as school teaching, especially elementary school teaching, is primarily a female profession in China, gender equality is a particularly important issue. Israel prohibits discrimination based on national origin, sex, or religion. Pursuant to Palestine's Amended Basic Law of 2003, all Palestinians shall be equal before the law and the judiciary, without any distinction based upon race, sex or gender, color, religion, political opinion, and/or disability, noting that positions are available on the basis of equal opportunity. Teachers in South Korea have the right to freedom from discrimination based on race, gender, disability, and/or religion.

Student Rights

Admissions and Freedom from Discrimination

All of the education law systems covered in this book have enacted compulsory attendance laws specifying the ages at which children must enter and through which they must remain in schools. In order to ensure fair and orderly admissions processes, many of these laws also set forth antidiscrimination provisions to protect children.

In China, while students cannot be discriminated against due to their religious beliefs or lack thereof, it is not clear whether and to what extent religious accommodations are provided in admissions and other aspects of schooling outside of autonomous ethnic areas. In Israel, discrimination based on national origin, sex, and/or religion is illegal. In Palestine, all children enjoy the right to education free from discrimination and are guaranteed places in school.

South Korea forbids discrimination against children in its multidimensional admissions process and as well as other aspects of school. South Korean law also has policies for special populations such as the children of overseas Koreans, foreigners, and refugees of North Korea

However, insofar as South Korea's major laws on education regulate only limited areas of student activities, they do not address topics discussed below such as freedom of speech, freedom of religion, and drug testing or searching students.

Freedom of Religion

As individual citizens, with the constitutional right to believe in, or not to believe in, any religion, students in China cannot be discriminated against due to their religious beliefs or lack thereof. Even so, it is unclear whether and to what extent religious accommodations are provided in Chinese public schools, especially in those outside of autonomous ethnic areas. Israel's Student's Rights Act does not explicitly address freedom of religion but its legal system has forbidden discrimination based on religion. Students in Palestine have the freedom to practice their religious beliefs through prayer and dress. Turkey's constitution grants all persons, including students, the right to freedom of conscience, religious belief, and conviction.

Freedom of Speech and Expression

The education law systems in the five nations reviewed in this volume vary with regard to speech and expression and the related matter of whether students must wear uniforms to school regardless of their religious beliefs. Although South Korea's Constitution provides for freedom of religion, as noted, its education laws do not address the rights of students to freedom of religion and speech. As noted, Palestinian students have the freedom to practice their religious beliefs through prayer and dress as well as to exercise their freedom of expression and opinion. Paradoxically, though, while the school disciplinary system in Palestine allows the failure to wear school uniforms to be considered a punishable offence, this strict dress code contradicts the freedom of expression laid out in the Basic Law.

In Turkey, students in primary and secondary schools are not required to wear uniforms but must be clean and tidy in their appearances. Females may wear headscarves at *Imam Hatip* secondary schools in all courses and in both in primary and secondary schools may wear headscarves in the elective course "the Quran." Even so, a prescriptive dress code sets out a variety of prohibitions such as against wearing shorts, tights, mini-skirts, slit skirts, short pants, sleeveless shirts and t-shirts, scarves, hats, bags, or other accessories displaying political symbols, and wearing makeup, having dyed hair, and growing mustaches and/or beards.

Due Process and Discipline

Palestine, South Korea, and Turkey have enacted extensive systems of due process safeguarding the rights of students who are subject to suspension and/or expulsion from school. Pursuant to Jordanian law governing parts of Palestine, although students cannot be expelled from school before completion of the tenth grade, exceptions are permitted for those who are mentally or physically ill. Corporal punishment is tolerated, unpunished, and mostly overlooked in Turkish schools while it is expressly forbidden in China and Israel.

China has an array of laws on discipline, and is increasingly relying on due process, but its national laws have not systematically articulated the conditions and procedures for student discipline in elementary and secondary education. Within this system, school officials in China are banned from expelling children who are in compulsory education, or the first nine years of schooling. Other than schools in its ultra-orthodox sector and NGO-controlled schools, Israeli law provides extensive due process protections when subject to discipline and or suspension and expulsion.

Search and Seizure/Drug Testing

Due to growing problems associated with violence coupled with the use of weapons, drugs, and alcohol in and around schools, some nations have addressed the need to search students and/or their property as well as to subject them to drug testing. China recognizes the freedom from unlawful searches. Even so, Chinese educators can, if necessary, search students and their property subject to governmental guidelines.

In order to ensure school safety, a variety of officials, including teachers, in Turkey may search buildings, desks, and other places to prevent improper student behavior from turning into crimes, to provide security of educational environments, and to protect students against improper and harmful behavior. Even so, regulations in Turkey do not address drug testing of students.

Students with Special Needs

In dealing with children with special needs, China protects the rights of children with disabilities by increasingly placing policy emphasis on inclusion, offering at least three different types of placements depending on the needs of individual students. In Israel the Special Education Act of 1988 protects the rights of children with disabilities. Similarly, Palestinian law provides all persons with special needs equal opportunities for education. However, the parental practice of tending to send their male, rather than their female, children with special needs to school explicitly violates the right of female students to receive an education. South Korean offers programming for children with special needs in elementary, middle, and high schools in both regular and special classes designed to prepare them for everyday life and social adaptation education.

Emerging Issues

In light of the rapid growth and development in technology, it should not be surprising that matters related to its use stands out as the primary emerging issue in the nations reviewed in this volume. Safety issues are gaining increased attention in China and Palestine. On other safety related matters, China has identified bullying as an emerging concern while South Korea has joined in the fight to prevent the growth of violence in schools. South Korea has introduced character education as a tool to help reduce violence and increase respect for educators. Also, South Korea is taking steps to introduce Nuri curricula to raise the quality of preschools for all children.

Meeting the educational needs of immigrant and refugee children from the war-torn regions in the Middle East as well as the conflicts on Turkey's southeast border present its educational and political leaders with major challenges. Further, Israel continues an emerging debate on the rights of students in schools. At the same time, Palestine is focusing on curricular developments and the related matter of entrance examinations testing students' knowledge as the single most important indicator of their ability to progress to the next academic stage. Rather than focus on reading comprehension and memorization, the Minister for Education and Higher Education proposed reforms to revolutionize education in Palestine by inviting more creative and interactive approaches to teaching and learning.

RECOMMENDATIONS

In light of the preceding summaries on the status of the national systems of education law described in this volume, it should be evident that schooling is a fundamental human right. As such, educational, political, and civic leaders not only in the nations reviewed in this volume, but elsewhere, must act to ensure the compulsory attendance rights for all children regardless of demographic characteristics such as race, gender, and religion.

To this end, leaders must focus on developing laws and implementing policies designed to improve schooling in places where compulsory attendance laws have long been in place. Accordingly, leaders may wish to consider the following recommendations that are designed to enhance the quality of schooling.

1. Consistent with the internationally accepted norms in the various covenants, leaders must take steps to have education explicitly recognized and safeguarded as a fundamental human right for all children. In other words, all nations must develop laws and policies designed to protect and enhance the rights of all students, and educators, regardless of their ethnicity, genders, race, and/or religion. Insofar as this can be a major challenge in parts of the world that have been reluctant to extend full rights to historically underrepresented groups such as women and religious and ethnic minorities, political and educational leaders in particular must show their mettle if they are to help their citizens to reach their full potential.
2. National and local leaders must work together to provide adequate funding designed to create schools wherein teachers can provide children with world-class educations. This is especially important during a time when there is a growing cynicism about the need for education such that it must move beyond concerns over resources or capacity in order to focus on how systems can not only be funded but also be made accessible to all. Equitable funding must cover not only construction of facilities and purchasing instructional materials but also paying salaries designed to enhance "the best and brightest" to enter

the field of education as teachers and administrators. Moreover, in making certain that all regions of a country receive adequate minimum levels of resources for schools, funding mechanisms should consider providing additional allocations for more expensive locales such as cities as well as for children with intensive needs including those with disabilities and/or those who speak minority languages and need to be taught in national/majority languages so that they can adapt in educational settings.

3. Education must be treated as an integrative factor, one that can help prepare all children to become productive members of their societies rather than set them apart from one another based on ethnicity, genders, race, and/or religion.
4. Reconceptualized school systems must be open to all children wherein educators emphasize pluralistic, cross-cultural principles that respect internationally accepted norms, as well as national laws, as explicated in the various covenants discussed herein. In other words, systems must be inclusive, not exclusive.
5. Laws and policies must be enacted to meet the needs of special student populations including, but not limited to, those who are disabled, of ethnic, religious, and linguistic minorities, and/or are refugees.
6. Institutions of higher learning must enhance teacher and administrator preparation programs, ensuring that they are at the "cutting edge" of school reform so that they can best help to educate children.
7. Leaders should adopt proactive roles in helping to create shared values among all groups in developing educational curricular/standards. It is essential for officials in central governmental ministries to maintain leadership roles in education to ensure that policies and practices are adopted uniformly in all schools and areas of their countries.
8. Educators must develop curricula, and accompanying texts, drafted primarily by appropriate professionals who can call on outside experts for assistance. Individuals from the respective governmental and educational ministries as well as from the higher education sector should provide leadership on this important project. Even as educational leaders work to develop curricula with an eye toward primarily satisfying what can be described as national needs, they must simultaneously challenge students to develop critical thinking skills befitting individuals who are preparing to assume roles as full citizens.
9. Leaders should implement curricula that all can accept. Educational leaders should also provide some consideration for ways of permitting minority and ethnic groups to preserve their independent heritages in the schools by being open to incorporating elements of their perspectives into curricula.

10. Members of committees assigned the task of developing curricular materials should be selected from among a broad representation of stakeholders, including, but not limited to parents, students, teachers, civic leaders, interested in helping to ensure equal educational opportunities for all children.
11. Leaders, particularly in developing nations, should schedule conferences/meetings on the right to schooling in an attempt to obtain input from all parties, again including, but not limited to parents, students, teachers, and civic leaders, who are interested in helping to ensure equal educational opportunities for all children. In developed nations, educational leaders in particular should encourage parents to become more involved in the education of their children and citizens to vote to ensure that their school boards or governing bodies truly represent community interests while holing to appropriate educational standards.
12. In light of the rapid pace at which change occurs, leaders should regularly reevaluate and update educational goals to keep them current.

CONCLUSION

As growing interdependence between and among nations shrinks the world community, a major challenge facing civic, educational, and political leaders is ensuring the educational rights of all children. Moreover, insofar as human dignity is closely related to the protection of the physical and mental well-being of students as they grow to become productive members of their societies, the quality of the education available to them is key to the reduction and elimination of adult illiteracy and poverty in future generations.

Given the importance that education has assumed in the twenty-first century, it all but goes without saying that improvements in basic schooling for all children are a prerequisite to sustainable personal and social development. In fact, individuals are ultimately unable to exercise their fundamental social, civil, economic, and political rights unless they have received an adequate basic education. To the extent that education is a lasting investment in the future of children, indeed of society itself, as well as sustainable development and social progress in general, it is critical to improving the lives of all helping them both to break the cycle of poverty and to lead lives of full participation in democratic societies.

In the words of the United States Supreme Court, insofar as "education is perhaps the most important function of state and local governments,"[1] it is imperative for civic, educational, and political leaders to ensure that the educational rights of students remain protected as a basic component of their fundamental human rights. As daunting as the crucial challenge of safeguarding educational rights may be, it is one all leaders should welcome as they seek to build a better tomorrow for all children and their societies at large.

Aware of the need for schooling, then, this book, and its companion volume, has striven to cover a wide array of aspects in the education laws in the K–12 systems in the five nations examined in this volume. Most nations recognize that students and teachers in general have legal rights to freedom from discrimination as well as to freedom of speech, religion, and association. Yet the legal systems in some of the countries restrict some of these rights to protect the public or national order.

The aim of this volume was to shed light on the rights, duties, and new challenges on education law systems while highlighting the importance of respecting education as a fundamental right. As such, I hope this book will contribute to and provide a new impetus in the debate on the status of K–12 education worldwide. Inspired by what the contributors have written, we hope that lawmakers, policymakers, and educational leaders can proceed to outline new visions of developments for the rights of students and teachers culminating in increased student achievement even if these changes are driven by national, rather than international, priorities.

NOTE

1. *Brown v. Board of Education*, 347 U.S. 483, 493 (1954).

Index

ACFTU. *See* All-China Federation of Trade Unions
ACRI. *See* Association for Civil Rights in Israel
Act on the Prevention and Countermeasures against Violence in Schools, 95
administration, 4
admissions, 128; discrimination and, 73; student rights and, 91–93, 113
All-China Federation of Trade Unions (ACFTU), 11
Amended Basic Law of 2003, 59; Article 4(2), 69; Article 24 of, 66, 67
Amim, Ir, 60
anti-discrimination law, 127; in Palestine, 73
apprenticeship, student rights and, 30
Arab-Palestinians, discrimination against, 31
Arafat, Yasser, 68
Ashkenazi Jews, 31, 33, 40
Association for Civil Rights in Israel (ACRI), 36, 40, 60
Atatürk, 104

Baccalaureate Programs, 6
Basic Law of National Education No. 1739, 107
Basic Laws (Knesset), 28, 40
Bedouin villages, 47
bianzhi, 8
Brighouse, H., 30

cell phone use, 16
character education, in South Korea, 96–97
Character Education Improvement Law, 99
Cheonbook Province, 90
childhood, 30
child labor, 3
China: compulsory education in, 3; discipline in, 8–9; dismissal in, 8–9; due process in, 14; education in, 1; education law in, 1, 2; emerging, 16–17; equal protection in, 11; establishment of employment in, 7–8; ethics in, 8–9; faculty rights in, 7–11; freedom of religion in, 15; funding in, 3; gender equality in, 12; government relationships in, 18–19; international schools in, 5–6; judicial rulings in, 18; licensure in, 7; minority students in, 12–13; population of, 1; private schools in, 4–5; public schools in, 19; safety issues in, 6; search and seizure in, 15; state and local relationships in, 17; student rights in, 12–16; substantive rights in, 9–10; tenure in, 22n51; vocational schools in, 4
Chinese Communist Party, 8, 10
Choi, Sheena, xiii
citizenship, student rights and, 30

Civil Servant Selection Examination, 110
Civil Service Law, 68; Article 2(1), 70; Article 23, 72
Commissions of Wise Men, 105
Comoglu, Irem, xiii
compulsory education, 124–125; in China, 3; in Palestine, 65–66; in South Korea, 82–87; in Turkey, 108
Compulsory Education Law (1986), 2; amendments to, 13; Article 11, 3; Article 35, 9
Compulsory Learning Act of 1939, 31
compulsory schooling laws, xii
conferences, 133
Constitution (Chinese), 10; Article 3, 17; Article 19, 2; education law and, 2; Fundamental Rights and Duties of Citizens in, 2
Constitution of the Republic of Turkey, 117
Continuing Education of Elementary and Secondary School Teachers (1999), 10
Convention on the Elimination of All Forms of Discrimination Against Women, 72
curricular development, 132–133; in Palestine, 75

Daoud, Akram, xiii
Declaration of Principles on Self-Government Arrangements, 53, 55
Declaration of United Nations Assembly Resolution 36/55 of 1981, 70
detainees, education of, 63–64
discipline, 129; in China, 8–9; due process and, 93–94; in Israel, 42–43; MOEHE on, 73; in South Korea, 93–94; student rights and, 93–94; in Turkey, 113–116
discrimination, 127, 128; admissions and, 73; in Israel, 40; student rights and, 33–34; Students' Rights Act 2000 and, 40–47
dismissal: in China, 8–9; due process and, 73–74; in South Korea, 88–89; in Turkey, 110–111
diversity, 34
drug testing, 130
dualist systems, 35
due process, 129; in China, 14; discipline and, 93–94; dismissal and, 73–74; in faculty rights, 126; in Palestine, 73–74; in South Korea, 88–89; in Turkey, 110–111

East Jerusalem: education law in, 60; enclaves, 56–57; MANHI in, 61; PNA in, 61; population of, 56; supervision systems in, 61
Eco-Friendly, 32
education: attainment, xii; in China, 1; of detainees, 63–64; in H2, 62; as human right, 131; outsourcing of, 38; in Palestine, 54–58; in Seam Zone, 62; in Turkey, 104–106; in West Bank, 62. *See also specific types and topics*
Education Bureau of Qingdao, 14
Education Development Strategy Plan, 62
education law: in China, 1, 2; Constitution (Chinese) and, 2; in East Jerusalem, 60; in Palestine, 53, 58–64; in Turkey, 106–107
Education Law (1995), 2, 13
Education Workers Union (KTU), 90
Elementary and Secondary Education Act (ESEA), 82, 91, 93; Article 13, 83; Article 18, 93; Enforcement Decree of, 93
equal protection: in China, 11; in Palestine, 71–72
ESEA. *See* Elementary and Secondary Education Act
establishment of employment, in China, 7–8
ethics: of care, 30; in China, 8–9
European Community, 104
expulsion, 114, 115–116; in Israel, 42–43

faculty rights: in China, 7–11; due process in, 126; in South Korea, 88–91; in Turkey, 110–111
fragile indicators, 62
Framework Act on Education, 89
freedom of association, 127; in Palestine, 70–71; in South Korea, 90–91; in Turkey, 112–113
freedom of religion, 127, 128; in China, 15; in Palestine, 70, 74; in South Korea,

90; in Turkey, 116
freedom of speech, 127, 129; in Palestine, 68–70; in South Korea, 89; in Turkey, 111–112
Freeman, M. D. A., 29
funding, 125; in China, 3; in Palestine, 66; for public education, 66

Gaza Strip, 53, 54, 75, 76
gender equality, in China, 11, 12
Gibton, Dan, xiii
GLTBQ, 36
governance, 125
governing boards, in Palestine, 66–67
government relationships, in China, 18–19
Green Line, 55, 57

H2, 57; education in, 62
Hamas, 55
Han ethnicity, 12
Haredi, 31
Hebron City, 54, 57, 64
hepatitis B virus, 11
higher education, 22n51, 132; in Palestine, 65
Higher Education Law No. 11 of 1998, 59, 71
Human Capabilities, Nussbaum on, 29
human capital theory approach, 30
human rights, education as, 131
Human Rights Council (HRC), 63
Huzhou, 20n16

immigrants, in Turkey, 118–119, 120
Independent Commission for Human Rights (ICHR), 68, 69
International Convention on the Rights of the Child, 29
International Covenant on Civil and Political Rights, Article 18, 70
international schools, in China, 5–6
Israel: demographics of, 31; discipline in, 42–43; discrimination in, 40; expulsion in, 42–43; founding, 27, 48; jurisdiction in, 42–43; legal system in, 27–28; privacy in, 42–43; student rights in, 29–37; teacher rights in, 37–39
Israeli High Court of Justice, 60
Israeli prisons, 58
ITU, 37

Jerusalem Municipal Education Authority (MANHI), 60; in East Jerusalem, 61
Jordanian Education Law, 73, 75; Article 5, 69; Article 25, 71
Jordan Valley, 55
judicial rulings, in China, 18
justice, 29

Kemal, Mustafa, 104
KFTA. *See* Korean Federation of Teachers' Association
kindergarten: MOEHE on, 65; in Palestine, 65
Knesset, 27, 35; Basic Laws, 28, 40; legislation of, 28
knowledge, student rights and, 30
Ko, Jang Wan, xiii
Korean Constitution, 89
Korean Federation of Teachers' Association (KFTA), 90
KTU. *See* Education Workers Union

Labor Contract Law, 8
Labor Law, 70, 71; Article 100, 72
Labour Law No. 7 of 2000, 60
Law of the Rights of the Disabled No. 4 of 1999, 72, 74
Law on Nation-wide Commonly-used Languages and Characters, 13
Law on the Promotion of Non-Public Schools (2002), 2, 4, 5, 21n31
Law on the Protection of Minors, 2
Law on the Protection of the Rights and Interests of Women, 12
Law on the Unification of Education in 1924, 105
legal system, 124; in Israel, 27–28; in Turkey, 106–107
liability, 126; in Palestine, 68
licensure, in China, 7
Lozano, Ricardo, xiii

MANHI. *See* Jerusalem Municipal Education Authority
Master teacher system, 88
maternity leave, 11
MEB. *See* Milli Eğitim Bakanlığı

migrant children, in China, 13–14
Military Order, 63
Milli Eğitim Bakanlığı (MEB), 105
minban schools, 4
Ministry of Detainees and Ex-Detainees' Affairs (MODEDA), 64
Ministry of Education (China), 4
Ministry of Education and Higher Education (MOEHE), 58, 61, 75; direction by, 67; on discipline, 73; Education Development Strategic Plan 2014-2019, 59; guidelines, 73; on kindergarten, 65; UNRWA and, 63
Ministry of Justice, 35–36
minority students, 23n101; in China, 12–13
MODEDA. *See* Ministry of Detainees and Ex-Detainees' Affairs
MOEHE. *See* Ministry of Education and Higher Education
monist systems, 35
monitoring systems, 74
mutuality, 30

National Council for the Child (NCC), 36
National Curriculum, 32
National Education Act 1953, 32, 43; Article 11, 32
National Education Basic Act of 1739, 105
National-Formal stream, 31
National People's Congress, 4
National-Religious stream, 31
NATO, 104
NCC. *See* National Council for the Child
negligence, in Palestine, 68
NGOs. *See* nongovernmental organizations
nondiscrimination, 40
nongovernmental organizations (NGOs), 32
non-public schools, in Palestine, 67
North Korea, 93
Nuri Curriculum, 125; in South Korea, 98
Nussbaum, M. C., on Human Capabilities, 29

open upper secondary high school, 110
Organization for Economic Cooperation and Development (OECD), 81
Oslo I, 53, 55, 64
Oslo II, 55, 56, 57
Ottoman Empire, 27, 104, 117

Palestine, 27, 53; anti-discrimination law in, 73; compulsory education in, 65–66; curricular development in, 75; due process in, 73–74; education in, 54–58; education law in, 53, 58–64; equal protection in, 71–72; freedom of association in, 70–71; freedom of religion in, 70, 74; freedom of speech in, 68–70; funding in, 66; governing boards in, 66–67; higher education in, 65; institutional issues, 64–68; kindergarten in, 65; liability in, 68; negligence in, 68; non-public schools in, 67; pre-school in, 65; primary education in, 65; refugee camps, 57; safety in, 68; secondary education in, 65; special needs students in, 74; student rights in, 72–75; teacher rights in, 68–72; technology in, 75; territory in, 54–58; unions in, 71; violence in, 74
Palestinian Central Bureau of Statistics (PCBS), 55
Palestinian Child Law No. 7 of 2004, 59; Article 37(1)(b), 65
Palestinian Independence Declaration, 70
Palestinian-Israeli students, 41, 48
Palestinian Legislative Council, 59, 124
Palestinian National Authority (PNA), 53, 54, 57, 61; in East Jerusalem, 61
Palestinian Teachers' Union, 71
Park, Hyowon, xiii
PCBS. *See* Palestinian Central Bureau of Statistics
PNA. *See* Palestinian National Authority
PPP. *See* public-private partnerships
pregnancy, 11
pre-school, in Palestine, 65
primary education: in Palestine, 65; in South Korea, 82
Primary School Education Law 6287, 108, 120
privacy, in Israel, 42–43
Private School Act, 89
private schools: in China, 4–5; for-profit, 5
promotion: in South Korea, 88–89; in Turkey, 110–111

Provisional Method on Periodical Registration of Elementary and Secondary School Teacher License (2013), 10
Provisions on Case Guidance, 2
public education, funding for, 66
Public Education Officials Act, 82, 88, 89
public figures, 10
public-private partnerships (PPP), 3
public schools: in China, 19; in Palestine, 67
Publishing and Copyright Law, Article 3, 69
Punishment Settlement Committees, 94
Pupils' Rights Act, 35

Quality Assurance Commission, 67

Ramallah, 55
Rawls, John, 29, 30
reasonable return, 5
Recognized Non-Formal Schools, 32, 33
Regulation 29072 for Pre-school and Primary Education Institutions, 113
Regulation 287578 for Secondary Education Institutions, 113, 114
religion. *See* freedom of religion
religious education, 28
right to education, 48; student rights and, 33–34; Students' Rights Act 2000 and, 40–47
Royal-Dawson, Lucy, xiii

safety, 126; in Palestine, 68
safety issues, in China, 6
Saidam, Sabri, 76
School Supervision Act of 1969, 31
Seam Zone, 57; education in, 62
search and seizure, 130; in China, 15; in Turkey, 116
secondary education, 114; in Palestine, 65; in South Korea, 82; in Turkey, 109
segregation, student rights and, 33–34
Separation Wall, 53, 56
Sephardi Jews, 31, 33, 40
SES. *See* socioeconomic status
sexual harassment, 9, 42, 74; students rights and, 12
Shandong, 14
shared values, 132
Shenzhen, 16
short-term suspensions, 115
social security, 24n114
socioeconomic status (SES), 31
SOE. *See* Superintendent of the Office of Education
South Korea, 81, 128; character education in, 96–97; compulsory education in, 82–87; discipline in, 93–94; dismissal in, 88–89; due process in, 88–89; emerging issues in, 95–99; faculty rights in, 88–91; freedom of association in, 90–91; freedom of religion in, 90; freedom of speech in, 89; institutional issues in, 82–87; Nuri Curriculum in, 98, 125; primary education in, 82; promotion in, 88–89; secondary education in, 82; special needs students in, 94–95; student rights in, 91–95; tenure in, 88–89; violence in, 95–96
special education, in China, 15–16
Special Education Act of 1988, 31
special needs students, 130, 132; in Palestine, 74; in South Korea, 94–95; in Turkey, 117
speech. *See* freedom of speech
SSTA, 37
state and local relationships, in China, 17
State Council, 4, 14
strikes, 71
student rights, 128–130; admissions and, 91–93, 113; apprenticeship and, 30; in China, 12–16; citizenship and, 30; discrimination and, 33–34; in Israel, 29–37; knowledge and, 30; in Palestine, 72–75; right to education and, 33–34; segregation and, 33–34; sexual harassment and, 12; sociopolitical background of, 31–32; in South Korea, 91–95; sub-groups, 30; teacher rights and, 37–39; in Turkey, 113–117; before 2000, 35
Students' Rights Act 2000, 27, 128; Article 1, 38, 39, 46; Article 3, 40, 46; Article 4, 40; Article 5, 40, 46; Article 5A, 40, 41; Article 5B, 42; Article 5C, 42; Article 6, 42; Article 7, 42; Article 8, 42; Article 10, 43; Article 11, 43;

Article 14, 43; articles of, 36; courts and, 44–47, 45; critique of, 43–44; discrimination and, 40–47; opposition to, 36; overview of, 36–37; rights in, 36–37; right to education and, 40–47; structure and content of, 37; Supreme Court on, 46–47; UNCRC and, 43–44
subjects, 30
substantive rights, in China, 9–10
Sunday School, 34
Superintendent of the Office of Education (SOE), 91
Supreme Court (Israel), 27, 28, 47; on Basic Laws, 28; on Students' Rights Act 2000, 46–47
Supreme Court (U.S.), 28, 133
Supreme People's Court, 2, 14
Syrian refugees, 118, 119

Tawjhi, 76
teacher rights: in Israel, 37–39; in Palestine, 68–72; student rights and, 37–39. *See also* faculty rights
teachers, job security of, 39
Teacher's Employment Examination, 88
Teachers Law (1993), 2, 7; Article 7, 9
Teaching Profession Career Ladder Program (TPCLP), 111
technology, in Palestine, 75
Tel Aviv District Court, 63
tenure: in China, 22n51; in South Korea, 88–89; in Turkey, 110–111
territory, in Palestine, 54–58
Tian Yong v. Beijing University of Science and Technology (1999), 14
TPCLP. *See* Teaching Profession Career Ladder Program
Turkey: compulsory education in, 108; conflict in, 117–118; discipline in, 113–116; dismissal in, 110–111; due process in, 110–111; education in, 104–106; education law in, 106–107; emerging issues in, 117–119; faculty rights in, 110–111; freedom of association in, 112–113; freedom of religion in, 116; freedom of speech in, 111–112; history of, 104; immigrants in, 118–119, 120; legal system in, 106–107; location of, 103; population of, 104; programs of study in, 109; promotion in, 110–111; search and seizure in, 116; secondary education in, 109; special needs students in, 117; student rights in, 113–117; tenure in, 110–111; vocational education in, 110
Turkish Grand National Assembly, 106–107
Turkish National Education System, 105, 107
Turkish Special Education Needs Legislation, 117

Ultra-Orthodox Jews, 31
UNCRC. *See* United Nations Convention on the Rights of the Child
unions, 36, 127; in China, 11; in Palestine, 71; in Turkey, 112–113
United Nations Convention on the Rights of the Child (UNCRC), 30, 37, 39, 59; ratification of, 35; Students' Rights Act 2000 and, 43–44
Universal Declaration on Human Rights, Article 26, xi
UN Relief and Works Agency for Palestinian Refugees in the Near East (UNRWA), 57, 63, 66; MOEHE and, 63

verbal warnings, 114
violence: in Palestine, 74; in South Korea, 95–96
vocational education, in Turkey, 110
Vocational Education Law (1996), 2, 4
vocational schools, in China, 4

West Bank, 53, 76, 77; Area A of, 55–56; Area B of, 55–56; Area C of, 55–56, 62; education in, 62
written censures, 114, 115

Yao, Jinju, xiii
Yükseköğretim Kurulu, 105

Zhang, Ran, xiii
Zhengzhou, 20n14
Zhongwei, 20n15

About the Editor

Charles J. Russo, MDiv, JD, EdD, is the Joseph Panzer Chair in Education in the School of Education and Health Sciences, director of its PhD program in educational leadership, and research professor of law in the School of Law at the University of Dayton. The 1998–1999 president of the (American) Education Law Association, and 2002 recipient of its McGhehey (Achievement) Award, he received a PhD Honoris Causa from Potchefstroom University, now the Potchefstroom Campus of Northwest University, in Potchefstroom, South Africa, in May 2004, for his contributions to the field of education law. Russo authored or coauthored more than 280 articles in peer-reviewed journals; authored, coauthored, edited, or coedited sixty-two books, including this volume, and more than 1,000 publications. He has spoken extensively on issues in education law in the United States and twenty-nine other nations.

About the Contributors

Sheena Choi, PhD, is associate professor of management at Indiana University–Purdue University Fort Wayne. She received her PhD in social foundations of education at the State University of New York at Buffalo and was a Fulbright Senior Research Fellow to South Korea during 2008–2009. She completed the Post-Doctoral Bridge to Business Program at the University of Florida, Gainesville, during the summer of 2016. Dr. Choi publishes extensively about internationalization of higher education, international education, and intersection of organization, cultural values, and education.

Akram Daoud, PhD, has been the dean of the Faculty of Law at An-Najah National University in Palestine since January 2008. After completing his studies in philosophy and law in France, Dr. Daoud started lecturing in the field of private law. He enjoys his time working in the education sector, specifically in legal education, as he believes it to be the tool of change in his country. Throughout his career, Dr. Daoud also has promoted new approaches and teaching methods within An-Najah National University in Palestine, furthering its expert position in legal education.

Lucy Royal-Dawson, PhD, is research associate at the School of Law, University of Ulster. Palestine was the focus of her doctoral study which looked at the legal obligations for the right to higher education in this situation of occupation where, in effect, there are two duty-bearers. She had previously lived there for two years, working at An-Najah National University for eighteen months. She has over thirty years of work experience in the education sector, and, in the last decade, has applied the human rights lens in her work in education.

Dan Gibton, PhD, MA, LLB, tenured associate professor of education policy and law, at the Constantiner School of Education, adjunct lecturer at the Buchmann Faculty of Law, Tel-Aviv University, Israel, and visiting professor at the London Centre for Leadership in Learning, UCL Institute of Education, London. His areas of interest include school reform, legislation and school reform, the nature and emergence of education law and law-based reform (mainly in Israel and England); and qualitative methods in policy studies.

Irem Comoglu, PhD, is associate professor at ELT Department at Dokuz Eylul University, Turkey. Her research interests are English language teacher education, teacher development, and qualitative research design.

Jan Wan Ko is chair and associate professor of higher education in the Department of Education and a director of the Center for Teaching and Learning at Sungkyunkwan University in Korea. He has served as a member of the Ministry of Education's Advisory Committee, a director-general of the Korean Association for Higher Education, and a Director of the Center for Institutional Effectiveness at Sungkyunkwan University. He holds a BA and an MA from Sungkyunkwan University and a PhD from University of Missouri–Columbia in the United States. His current research interests focus on the internationalization of higher education, institutional effectiveness, and financing higher education. His publications focusing on those areas appear in many recognized journals including *Educational Policy* and the *Journal of Korean Education.*

Ricardo Lozano, PhD, is an assistant professor in the College of Education at Concordia University Texas in Austin; he formerly was at Hasan Kalyoncu University in Gaziantep, Turkey. His research interests are in the areas of comparative education, education and international development, and teacher preparation programs internationally. He is a graduate of Texas A&M University with a PhD in education administration and international economic development and a graduate of Concordia University, Texas, with an MEd in curriculum development and instruction.

Hyowon Park is a PhD candidate in the Educational Theory and Policy program and also in the Comparative and International Education program at Pennsylvania State University. She has participated in conducting teacher policy research as a research assistant at the Office of Teacher Policy Research, Primary and Secondary Education Research Division in Korean Educational Development Institute (KEDI), one of the leading institutions in educational policy development and its implementation. Her dissertation explores the role of teacher unions on teacher policy development and transformation processes, especially with the case of teacher evaluation for professional development policy in South Korea. Park hopes to connect her research on legislators to impact teacher policies.

Jinju Yao is associate professor of educational law in the Law School and deputy director of Human Resources Division, Beijing Foreign Studies University, China. She received her LLB and LLM from Northwest University of Political Science and Law in 1999 and 2002, PhD in law from China University of Political Science and Law in 2005. She has published many papers on Chinese and American educational law. In addition, she has participated in drafting and amending education law and policies at national level while creating a center for education law in Beijing Foreign Studies University as executive director and has hosted the Education Law Forum every year since 2011. Yao has received research grants from the Ministry of Education, P.R.C. and currently is vice chair of the Education Law Association of Beijing Law Society. Her research interests include education law, global governance, and public law.

Ran Zhang is associate professor of educational law in the Graduate School of Education, Peking University, China. She received an LLB from Peking University in 2000 and a PhD in Educational Policy Studies from Indiana University in 2009. Zhang has published many articles and book chapters on Chinese or American educational law, and her dissertation won the CIES (Comparative and International Education Society) Higher Education Special Interest Group Best Dissertation Award (2009–2010). Her research interests include educational law, comparative education, and research methodology.

www.ingramcontent.com/pod-product-compliance
Lightning Source LLC
Chambersburg PA
CBHW021601210326
41599CB00010B/539
* 9 7 8 1 4 7 5 8 3 9 5 4 8 *